Treasure Island, the Panto

A pantomime

Richard Lloyd

Samuel French — London

New York - Toronto - Hollywood

TREASURE ISLAND, THE PANTO

First performed as *Panto Walks the Plank* by Theatre Workshop Coulsdon on Saturday, 9th December 1995 at Coulsdon Youth and Social Centre, with the following cast:

THE QUALITY

Squire Polperro	Timothy Young
The Honourable Nancy Polperro	Kimberley Argles
Dr Liversausage	Christopher Argles
Captain Smellit	Bruce Montgomery

THE SCUM OF THE SEVEN SEAS

Billy Fishbones	Derek Crouch
Long John Slither	Neil Grew
Pink Dog	Lisa Lloyd
Blind Puke	Paul M Ford
Israel Feet	Peter Bird
George Merry	Matthew Marsh
Seamus "Groundbait" O'Flaherty	Daniel Ireson

T'OTHERS

Jim Ladd	Claire Andreadis
Mrs Ladd	Michael Brown
Bodmin	Paul Breden
Newquay	Simon Crouch
Bertha Gunn	Tina Bretman
Captain Haddock	Penelope Simeone

LOS ESPAGNOLS

Don Iguana Del Anaconda Con Queso	Richard Lloyd
Donna Estella Del Torremolinos y Chimichanga	Victoria Gunstone

Assorted pirates, belike Tatiana Alison, Jonathan Wales, Elaine Marsh, Caitriona Farrell, Laura Morley, Ross Dunleavy, Sean Young

UPON THE QUARTER DECK

The Skipper (Director) Richard Lloyd
The First Mate (Assistant Director: shanties, jigs and suchlike) Tatiana Alison
The Bosun (Moosical Director, d'ye see?) Mark Taylor
Ship's Carpenter (Technical Director) Mark Hobbs

YE OLDE CAST OF CHARACTERS,
BY THUNDER, AND YE MAY LAY TO THAT

Billy Fishbones, an inebriated old ex-pirate
Jim Ladd, a brisk young spark, and principal boy
Mrs Ladd, Jim's mum and pantomime dame
Dr Liversausage, a seafaring quack
Squire Polperro, Oons sirrah! An archetypal product of the public school
    system
The Honourable Nancy Polperro, Squire Polperro's adorable daughter,
    and principal girl
Newquay ⎫
Bodmin ⎭ the Squire's faithful (but completely useless) lackeys
Captain Smellit, a taciturn sea captain
Long John Slither, a charming (but wholly untrustworthy) amputee, ha ha!
Captain Haddock, a Guatemalan crimson parakeet
Israel Feet, a pirate
Seamus "Groundbait" O'Flaherty, an Irish buccaneer
Blind Puke, a visually-challenged pirate
Pink Dog, a thoroughly villainous female pirate
George Merry (who isn't), a pirate
Don Iguana Del Anaconda Con Queso, His Most Catholic Excellency, the
    Spanish Ambassador to Guadeloupe
Donna Estella Del Torremolinos y Chimichanga, a sumptuous Hispanic
    beauty
Bertha Gunn, a potty old ex-pirate and tea lady
Other assorted **Pirates**, belike

SYNOPSIS OF SCENES

SONGS AND MUSIC

The original production ran for two hours and fifteen minutes including a fifteen minute interval. If this duration is deemed too long, songs number 2 and 10 (solos for Jim and Donna Estella respectively) may be omitted without undue detriment.

In addition to the songs listed, a good deal of incidental music is called for (indicated throughout the script), and will help any production along enormously.

ACT I

No. 1   Slither (Fifteen Men — traditional)
No. 2   Jim
No. 3   Slither and Pirates
No. 4   Nancy
No. 5   Slither and Pirates
No. 6   Dame
No. 7   The Company
No. 8   The Company

ACT II

No. 9   Pirates
No. 10   Donna Estella
No. 11   Audience participation song with Bertha, Nancy and Dame
No. 12   Jim and Donna Estella
No. 13   The Company
No. 14   The Company

A licence issued by Samuel French Ltd to perform this play does not include permission to use any copyright music. Where the place of performance is already licensed by the PERFORMING RIGHT SOCIETY a return of the music used must be made to them. If the place of performance is not so licensed then application should be made to the Performing Right Society, 29 Berners Street, London W1.

A separate and additional licence from PHONOGRAPHIC PERFORMANCES LTD, Ganton House, Ganton Street, London W1 is needed whenever commercial recordings are used.

PREFACE

Whilst *Treasure Island*, that perennial favourite of British children since its first publication, may seem an obvious candidate for panto treatment, actually arriving at a well-rounded pantomime, incorporating all the essential elements of that genre, whilst also sticking fairly strictly to the plot and characters of Stevenson's great novel, does pose a few problems!

So whilst the present script gets underway as a close pastiche of *Treasure Island,* you will notice it change tack part way through, in order to accommodate a boarding party of pirate clichés inspired by a wider literature.

Any fan of the Hollywood pirate epics of the 30s and 40s will tell you that *Treasure Island*, indisputably the most famous adventure in English literature, is nonetheless fatally flawed as a pirate story. For one thing, there's absolutely no love interest! In fact there are no women at all. (With the honourable exception of Mrs Hawkins — who is written out of the plot by page 27!)

Now, no good pirate movie is truly complete without the love interest — usually represented by Maureen O'Hara. Nor without the leering presence of the rascally Spaniards.

In fact, these two elements are so quintessential, that they are habitually combined through the well-worn cinematic device of "Swashbuckling hero falls for wicked Spanish Governor's haughty (but gorgeous) daughter — whom he has inadvertantly taken captive, the handsome dog!"

There are other important omissions from *Treasure Island* which undermine its credentials as a bona fide, all round pirate story. For instance, absolutely nobody walks the plank!

Now as it happens, nobody ever *did* walk the plank — Pirate buffs will tell you that this infamous punishment was simply a macabre whimsy of our Victorian ancestors, with their overheated imaginations. However, if you're indulging in a blood and thunder tale of skullduggery upon the high seas, you *expect* to see people walking the plank — it's part of the tradition.

The requirements of pantomime also necessitate other minor diversions from the real *Treasure Island* — nobody is horribly murdered for one thing. Gratuitous violence is purely of the slapstick variety!

You will also notice that the names of most characters have been altered slightly. Thus, Israel Hands becomes Israel Feet, Dr Livesey becomes Dr Liversausage, Smollett, Smellit, and so on. I must confess to experiencing certain prickings of conscience about tinkering with the names of some of the most famous (and infamous) characters in English literature. If this was just an excuse for cheap gags based on the comic potential of silly names, it would probably be unforgivable.

The truth however, is that this spoof is by no means the real *Treasure Island*, and all the characters differ in certain respects from their progenitors. A greater sin would have been to trivialize Stevenson's consummately three-dimensional originals, by trying to locate them in a genre as frivolous as pantomime.

Of course, Long John's famous parrot serves perfectly as a pantomime animal — it even talks! And a "crimson parrot" does have a certain resonance with a particularly awful 1950s B-movie starring Burt Lancaster, and rejoicing in the title *The Crimson Pirate*. (Yes, it was filmed in "Glorious Technicolor".)

In conclusion, I must acknowledge the works of George Farquhar as my principal source for the copious supply of genuine eighteenth-century imprecations. What a shame no-one ever uses colourful and inoffensive expletives like "Oons!" "Garzoon!" or "Rat me!" any more.

Mind you, they probably *were* offensive at the time ...

Richard Lloyd

Other titles by Richard Lloyd
published by Samuel French Ltd

A Christmas Cavalier
Smut's Saga, or Santa and the Vikings

To Morgan

ACT I

Overture

The corner of a darkened snug

Outside, the wind howls and rain lashes down. A single candle gutters fitfully on top of an upturned barrel, casting an unearthly glow on to a ring of villainous faces. A whispering voice is crooning in the near darkness

Song 1 (Slither)

Slither   Fifteen men, on a dead man's chest,
                     Yo ho ho! And a bottle of rum!
                     Drink and the Devil had done for the rest,
                     Yo ho ho! And a bottle of rum!

Ay ... I were there when he went ashore, lads. Him, the treasure chest, and six strong sailormen to carry it. 'Twas first light they made landfall. And at dusk, back comes the cap'n — and all alone. And the six strong sailormen all dead and buried ... Not a man Jack aboard could work out how he done it — nor where he buried that treasure. But done it he had, and made a map into the bargain. And that, my lads, I means to have. Come hell or high water I'll have Squint's map — or my name ain't Long John Slither! Ha ha ha ha!

Audience participation as the wicked laughter gradually dies away, drowned out by thunder, lightning, and storm effects. The candle is extinguished, and Lights fade to Black-out

Outside "The Admirable Bimbo Inn", somewhere in the west country

A creaking inn sign overhead depicts said bimbo

Jim Ladd, a rather prepossessing youth, enters. He whistles a merry seafaring tune as he goes about his chores, chalking up the chef's special on the blackboard beside the inn doorway

Jim (*to himself*) Now then, let's see, today's special, what have we got? (*Glancing at a piece of paper*) Fisherman's pie, or — nothing. Just the same as all the other days in fact. (*He sings*)

Song 2 (Jim)

A beautiful young lady, gorgeously attired, and of manifest quality enters. It is Nancy, lovely young daughter of Squire Polperro

Nancy Jim!
Jim Nancy!
Nancy Oh Jim!
Jim Oh Nancy, you shouldn't have come. Your father will be livid if he finds out.
Nancy Oh devil take Father! I just had to come, Jim. I had to see you.
Jim But you know he doesn't think I'm a suitable match. What with my mother owning this ramshackle pot house — and your father owning the entire county.
Nancy I don't care about that, Jim. Let's run away together. We'll take ship for the Spanish Main, to find love, honour, and to make our fortunes.
Jim Yes, well — that's all very well for you to say. You've already got a fortune to come back to. All I'd have to fall back on would be a cold plate of fisherman's pie!
Nancy (*completely carried away*) Oh Jim! Fisherman's pie needn't stop us. Think of it! The adventure. The passion. The romance ...

Music swells up to introduce a hugely over-the-top romantic number — forestalled just in the nick of time by a gravelly shout from off stage

Gruff voice (*off*) Belay that row!
Nancy Someone's coming! I must away! (*She kisses his cheek*) Farewell, sweet Jim — until tonight ...
Jim Tonight! But Nancy, I'm not sure that I want to ... Oh bother.

She flees off R

Moments later, Billy Fishbones, a decrepit old nut-brown seafarer, enters L, *sporting the ubiquitous tarry pigtail, and dragging a monster sea chest behind him*

Billy Ahoy there! Shipmate! Lend an 'and will 'ee?

Readers will quickly come to identify all pirates or ex-pirates by this distinctive mode of speech, featuring a characteristic excess of apostrophes

Jim Of course, sir. Let me help you with that trunk.

Billy Aaar. That be right kind of 'ee, shipmate. Thank 'ee kindly. Now then, what manner o' place might this be, as I've fetched up in?

Jim Oh. You haven't fetched up have you, sir? I'll get a mop.

Billy Just answer the question, laddie — I'll do the gags.

Jim Fair enough. Well ... erm ... actually, it's an inn — *The Admirable Bimbo*.

Billy Shiver me timbers! Ye don't say! Why now, here's a stroke o' luck! For it just so happens, as I needs a berth to rest me weary old sea-legs for a while, somewhere I won't be disturbed by no — unwelcome callers. D'ye follow?

Jim Er, well, not really no ...

Billy Never mind! Now tell me, lad — what h'accomodation d'ye have available?

Jim Hold on. I'll have to find out. (*Calling*) Mother! Mother!

Dame (*off*) Coming!

Billy (*while they're waiting*) What name d'ye go by, lad?

Jim Jim.

Billy Aaar. Jim ... Jim lad.

Jim That's right.

Billy Eh?

The Dame enters, carrying a tray of steaming fisherman's pies

Dame Oh there you are, Jim. I just had to bring these pies out to develop a nice crust ... Well, what is it? Ooooh! I say! Company! Hallo sailor! And look, Jim! All these people! How unexpected! (*To the audience*) Ahoy there, mateys!

Audience titters nervously

Oh now come on! Let's try that again! I say: "Ahoy there mateys!", and you *don't* say: "Oh ruddy hell, they want us to join in" — no, you say: "Avast behind!" Then I do this visual gag see ... (*She turns around and bends over to flash her enormous bloomers at them*) A vast behind — geddit?

Boom Boom! — Groans likely

Yes, well, I feel the same way, dears, but it's better to get it over and done with at the beginning of the show. Saves cracking the same crummy gag all the way through. Right then! Let's try again shall we? Here we go then, after three — One. Two. Three! (*Bellowing*) Ahoy there, mateys!

Audience Avast behind!

Dame duly flourishes her bottom at them

Dame Right. Good. Thank heavens we've got that out of the way! Here! I
know! Let's just try a couple of other things while I've got your attention.
I call this my "audience participation workout". Also known as rabble-
rousing! Just to get you in the mood for the rest of the evening! Let's start
with some cheering, shall we? Here we are, Jim, strike a pose, dear.

Jim slaps his thigh. The audience cheer weakly

Oh blimey! I said *cheering*, not *jeering*. Let's try again. After three. One.
Two. Three.

Jim slaps his thigh again. The audience cheer more convincingly

Very good — Mr Motivator, eat your heart out! All right, let's try *booing*.
One. Two. Three.

The audience boo

Oh, spot on. Hissing?

The audience hiss

Clapping?

The audience clap

Well, you won't be doing that again tonight! Oh you're very good at this,
aren't you? Tell you what, you're so good, I'm going to let you be in the
play! Yes! You can play the part of Mob — this is the eighteenth century
after all! Oh, it'll be just like being at *Les Misérables!* Well, not quite the
same as *Les Misérables,* I must admit — but then, these aren't West End
prices, are they? Now then, where were we ... Ah yes. (*Turning back to Billy
Fishbones*) Hallo sailor, care to step inside and heave to?
Jim He's already "fetched up", I don't think he needs to "heave to" as well.
Billy (*ignoring Jim*) Top o' the day t'ye, mum. Might an old seafaring man
make so bold as to enquire after your name?
Dame He might, and don't call me mum.
Billy Well, what is it then?
Dame Mrs Ladd.
Billy I see ... And your son is ——?
Dame Jim Ladd.

Billy Of course.

Dame And my husband — Jim's father, Gawd rest his soul — was ——

Billy (*hazarding a guess*) Mr Ladd?

Dame S'right.

Billy Don't tell me — Alan?

Dame Nope. Jack. Well, Jack *The* actually.

Billy Jack the Ladd ... Oh yes, o'course. I knowed him right well.

Dame Did you really? (*Aside*) Blimey! That's more than I did. Anyway Mr ——?

Billy Fishbones — Billy Fishbones, at your service, mum.

Dame Well Mr Fishbones, what can I do for you?

Billy (*conspiratorially*) Board. Lodgin'. That head out there to watch ships off. And no questions asked.

Dame How much?

Billy Five gold pieces. In a h'advance.

Dame Done.

They spit on their palms and shake on it

Jim, take his trunk up. Room number seven. It's not *en-suite* I'm afraid, but you know what it's like this time of year — sails conferences and so on. (*To the audience*) *Sails* conferences, see? *SALES* conferences ... It's a joke! Oh, never mind.

Billy (*to Jim*) Wait up, lad. Afore ye go, I want to ask a favour of ye. Keep a weather eye open for a seafarin' man with only one leg. An' if you should spy him out, you comes for me first, understand me?

Jim Perfectly, sir.

Billy Aaar. Good boy, good boy. Here's a bright threepenny-bit for ye. And another every week, if ye keep your eyes skinned for that one-legged devil. Now then. Grog!

Jim I'm sorry?

Billy Grog! Grog, ye swab! Fetch me a mug o' grog, lad!

Jim Er, I don't think we keep that, sir. How about a G and T?

Billy Nar. I needs a man's drink! Got 'ny Campari and soda?

Jim Oh yes, sir.

Billy Wi' a slice o' lemon, and one o' they little umbrellies?

Jim Absolutely.

Billy Right. That'll do.

They go into the inn, lugging the sea chest between them

Dame (*to the audience*) Grog? Swabs? Seafaring men with one leg? I don't think I like the sound of this! (*She turns to pick up the tray of fisherman's pie*)

Bodmin and Newquay, two liveried footmen, enter

Oh hallo. More visitors. Now what?

Bodmin Good-day to you, my good woman.

Dame Oh. It's you. Hallo, Mr Bodmin. Have you come for your usual? (*nudging him*) — only I'm a bit busy as it goes ... guests, swabs, and so on.

Bodmin (*flustered*) No, ma'am. I regret I'm here upon business, not — pleasure.

Dame Oh, shame.

Newquay (*inquisitive*) What's "the usual"?

Bodmin Never you mind.

Newquay No — what? Go on. Tell me.

Dame (*holding up the tray*) Fisherman's pie of course. What did you think?

Newquay Doesn't matter.

Bodmin (*importantly*) We are sent to relay a missive to you from his worship, Squire Polperro.

Dame Oh yes?

Newquay (*unrolling a lengthy parchment*) It reads as follows: (*reading*) "Madam. Keep your ill-bred guttersnipe of a brat away from my noble daughter or I'll have him flogged through the shire and transported. Signed, George Polperro, MP, JP, etc., etc."

Dame Is that it?

Newquay (*nervously*) Er ... Yes.

Dame Well, can't say fairer than that, can you?

Newquay (*relieved*) No. Very generous of the squire I thought.

Bodmin Absolutely. Any chance of that fisherman's pie now?

Dame No. Bog off.

Bodmin But I thought ——

Dame (*exploding*) You think you can come down here and threaten me, and I'm going to feed you up on my best dogfish pie by way of a thank you? All right — you want one? (*To the audience*) Shall I? Shall I!

Audience participation. The Dame splurges a dish of fisherman's pie into Bodmin's face

Squire Pol-ruddy-perro! It's his hoity-toity little madam of a daughter who's pesterin' my Jim! Who does he think he is anyway? Does he think he owns the place?

Newquay He does own the place. He owns everything for fifty miles in any direction.

Dame Well not this inn he don't, so there! Now buzz off!

She goes inside and slams the door behind her

Newquay and Bodmin stand looking at each other — Bodmin blinking through a mask of mashed potato

Newquay (*after a pause*) Well, I think that went rather well.
Bodmin Oh, shut up.

Bodmin splats the other fisherman's pie in Newquay's face, and stomps off

The Lights fade down. In the Black-out "The Admirable Bimbo" inn sign is turned around to display out "The Spyglass Inn"

SCENE 2

The taproom of "The Spyglass Inn", Bristol Docks

The Lights come up on the Pirates, which include Israel Feet, George Merry and Groundbait, and Long John Slither, a charming but wholly untrustworthy amputee with a crutch

Raucous music leads into a pirate dance number with much swinging around, whooping, waving of cutlasses, and banging of tankards

As the music ends, Blind Puke enters, dressed in beggar's tatters, his eyes bandaged with a filthy rag, and accompanied by the tapping of his white stick

Blind Puke Ahoy there! Long John!
Slither I'm here. What news, Puke?
Blind Puke Not a blessed sign of him anywhere, John — He's clean vanished, and the map with him.
Slither T'ain't possible, shipmate. No man vanishes. We'll find him before many tides, and you may lay to that! And when we do, why, Billy Fishbones is as good as shark bait! Ha ha ha ha!

Audience participation

Well, well. Look 'ee here. 'Tis an unruly mob. They reminds me o' nothing so much as an abundance of plankton!

Audience participation

Oho! Now that ain't nice, is it?

He manages to look hurt and may even attract a few "aaahs"

Taking the rise out o' a man wi' only one leg? T'ain't right, shipmates. T'ain't proper. Not to pick on a disabled man ...

Pause. A wicked grin spreads slowly across his face

Ha ha ha! Well! That made you stop and think, didn't it? Shut you up for a minute. Ha ha ha! Oh, don't you waste no sympathy on me, shipmates, for I've twice the mischief in me as any two-legged man — as you shall presently see! Ha ha ha! Here now, why don't I interduce ye to the rest o' the crew. As likely a parcel o' rogues as ye may never wish to meet on a dark night! Ha ha ha!

He clumps along the line of glowering pirates, stopping first next to Blind Puke

This here is Blind Puke. Blind — for like me, he sacrificed his own good health for the sake o' King George, God bless him. Puke — because in twenty years before the mast, he never did find his sea legs! Ha ha ha!

The Pirates guffaw and jostle Puke. Slither moves along to Israel Feet

And this here is Israel — Israel Feet — on account o' his paddles stinkin' worse than a barrel o'ripe Gorganzola!

He passes along to George Merry

This is George. We calls him George Merry — 'cos he isn't! Ha ha ha!

The Pirates hoot and jostle at Merry who continues to glower. Slither reaches the end of the front row

And Seamus O' Flaherty so 'tis, also known as Groundbait. For he can't hold his grog upon the billow.

Slither gives Groundbait a shove and sends him sprawling

Oh and many more, shipmates. Too noomerous to mention. But every man jack o' them a' burstin' to get their flippers on Billy Fishbones' worthless neck! Ha ha ha! And we'll have him soon enough, don't you worry. For I'll have you know, that I've put my best man on the job — in a manner o'speakin'. Ha ha ha!

Audience participation

Oh come now, shipmates. As ye're along for the voyage, ye might as well throw in your lot wi' the side that's goin' to win out in the end! And that's us! Oh yes it is!

Audience participation

Pirates Oh yes it is!

Audience participation

Slither Come on, lads! Let's show these lubbers what's what, eh? We'll tread the Devil's measure! Dance, you maggoty dogs! Dance!

Song 3 (Slither and Pirates)

Music strikes up, and the dance begins again, the Pirates whooping and leaping like madmen

The Lights fade to Black-out

SCENE 3

The sparsely furnished saloon of "The Admirable Bimbo Inn"

A set of steps lead up to a second level, where the sea chest stands

Downstairs, Billy Fishbones is sprawled in his now customary chair, waving an empty tankard about

Jim enters

Billy Grog, lad! Grog!
Jim Still haven't got any grog I'm afraid, Cap'n. How about another large vodka-Martini?
Billy Blindin'!

The Dame enters to sweep the floor

Dame (*to Jim*) What does Captain Bird's-Eye want this time?

Jim Another drink I'm afraid.

Dame Bloomin' heck! He must be more soused than a bucket of pilchards by now! He's been here three ruddy weeks! And he stopped paying after the first three days! This has got to stop, Jim. 'Ere, go and tell him to sling his hook.

Jim He hasn't got a hook. You're thinking of that pirate from Peter Pan.

Dame (*in his normal voice*) Listen. I'll do the gags. Stick to the script.

Jim Fair enough.

Dame Well go on then.

Jim But he's dangerous when he's had a skinful — and he's armed to the teeth as usual.

Dame Oh I can't help that. He's guzzlin' me out of house and home. He's frightened off all me regular customers.

Jim It's the cursing and swearing that does it.

Dame It's not. It's his ruddy singing!

Billy (*bawling tunelessly*) "Fifteen men on a dead man's chest!"

Dame Oh Gawd! He's off again.

Billy Yo-ho-ho! (*Bellowing*) And a vodka-Martini!

Jim (*shouting*) Just coming. I'd better nip round to the out-house to get another bottle.

Dame (*gloomily*) Great.

Pink Dog enters, a thoroughly villainous looking person of the female gender, swaggeringly attired in piratical fashion — in various shades of shocking crimson

As Jim is about to step outside, he encounters her

Pink Dog Ahoy there! Shipmate!

Jim Yes, miss?

Pink Dog Ms.

Jim Sorry.

Pink Dog Come here, sonny. Is my old cully Bill Fishbones a-stayin' at this here inn?

Jim Er ... Hang on a minute ...

Pink Dog What are you doing?

Jim Just counting your legs: one, two — that's all right then. Yes, he is.

Pink Dog Well shiver me timbers! I've caught up with the old rogue at last.

Jim Would you like to see him?

Pink Dog Bring me alongside, matey.

Jim stares blankly at her for a moment, then realizing what she means, leads her across to where Billy is slumped in his chair. Pink Dog peers into Billy's bleary eyes

Bill? Come, Bill — you recognize an old shipmate surely?

The effect is electric. Billy is on his feet in an instant

Billy Pink Dog!
Pink Dog Ha ha! And who else?! Pink Dog indeed, Bill. As ever was. Come
for to look up my old cully, at *The Admirable Bimbo Inn*!
Jim *(to the Dame)* What's a cully?
Dame Search me.
Billy What d'ye want with me?
Pink Dog You know well enough, Bill. You've taken something that don't
entirely belong to you ——
Dame Too right he has. The whole stock of my bloomin' bar for one thing.
Pink Dog — our entitlement, Bill. As you stole from all us lads. And now
I'll take it back, nice an' quiet like — unless you'd rather swing for it! *(She
draws out her cutlass)*
Dame Oi! None of that! This is a respectable pub. I won't have no brawling
in my bar!

Billy sweeps out his cutlass

Billy If it comes to swinging — then swing all, says I!

*He goes for her. They fight furiously, but Billy (sadly out of condition) is
mortally wounded. The Dame manages to separate them with her broom, and
drives Pink Dog back and out*

Pink Dog goes

Dame Right! That's it. That is absolutely it! I've had just about enough of
you. Now out! Go on! Hoppit! *(Turning to Billy)* And as for you — you're
barred!
Jim Mum! I think he's wounded!
Dame Get off! He's just shamming. He's after another free drink.
Jim There's blood on the carpet.
Dame Blood! On my nice clean shagpile? Right! That does it! Go on, hoik
him out.
Jim Wait! You can't just throw him out like that.
Dame No. You're right. We'll take his money, then we'll throw him out.
Jim No! We must get help. I'll run for Doctor Liversausage.
Billy *(semi-conscious)* Doctors is all swabs!
Dame Yes, but wealthy swabs. *(To Jim)* I'll get his stuff.

They rush in different directions

The Dame exits

Jim bumps straight into none other than Blind Puke

Jim Oh! Sorry. My fault.
Blind Puke Aaarh. I hears a voice. A young voice. Will you give me your
hand, my dear child, and lead a poor blind man to a glass o' Jamaicy rum.
Jim Of course — yow!

He yelps as Blind Puke grabs him in an armlock

Blind Puke Now, you young villain! Take me to the cap'n, or I'll give you
a, er — a Chinese burn, so I will.
Jim But he's not well. In fact, he's not receiving visitors.
Blind Puke Oh. He'll see me right enough. I've got something for him, d'ye
see. Now you lead me up to him and say: "Bill, Bill, here's an old friend
for you, Bill."
Jim (*reciting*) Bill, Bill, here's an old friend, blah blah blah ... yep — got it.
Blind Puke Right then — tramp, my lad!

They approach Billy Fishbones, now comatose at his table

Jim (*trying to remember*) Bill, Bill, here's an old flame that wants to ... I'm
sorry, what was it again?

Billy Fishbones looks up and squeaks with abject terror

Blind Puke Now you sit where you are, Bill. Boy, take his wrist and bring
it near mine.

*Jim does as he is told. Blind Puke presses a piece of paper into Billy's hand
and closes the old pirate's horny fist about it*

There now. That's done.
Billy (*peering dubiously at the paper*) That's a till receipt from Tesco's (*or
other local supermarket*).
Blind Puke Is it? (*He lifts his eye bandage to look*) Oh bum. Well, have that
instead then. (*He snatches back the first scrap of paper and stuffs a different
piece into Billy's hand*)

Blind Puke scuttles nimbly off, tap-tapping his way off stage

Billy stares numbly at the paper, then starts trembling violently

Billy (*hamming terribly*) No! No! Not the Pink Spot!

Jim What is it, Cap'n?

Billy (*wheezing and rattling horribly*) 'Tis certain death, lad. I'm done for, sure as night follows day. And I don't have long neither! But we'll daddle 'em, Jim. We'll daddle 'em yet!

Jim We will?

Billy Oh ay. We'll daddle 'em. You go and get help, lad. Fetch soldiers. Tell 'em that they'll lay 'em aboard at *The Admirable Bimbo*. All Squint's crew.

Jim (*fascinated*) Who's Squint?

Billy Squint! Ha ha! The most bloodthirsty buccaneer ever to rove the Spanish Main! An' wi' a wicked passion for chocolate buttons.

Jim Chocolate buttons?

Billy Oh ay. Nothin' he liked better than choccy — 'cept pillagin'. I 'member him at the sackin' of Acapulco ... the whole blessed town in flames ... poor devils a-swingin' high from the gibbet, and that monster Squint wi' choccy smeared around his gob, roaring: "How's that for a game o' Spanish conkers, my lads!" I was his first mate I was. It's my old sea chest they're after, Jim. For I'm the only one as knows the place where the treasure is buried!

Jim Treasure, Cap'n!

Billy Treasure, lad! Come, give me your arm. We'll daddle 'em, Jim! We'll dadd — aaark! (*He clutches his throat, keels over and dies*)

Jim Mother! Mother!

The Dame runs on

Dame What? What?

Jim He's snuffed it.

Dame What? Hopped the twig? Oh marvellous. Now we'll have the ruddy health and hygeine inspectors in — all sorts of nosey blinkin' Parkers.

Jim No! Listen! It's buried treasure, Mother! That's what it's all about! Pirates and such! We need the key to his old sea chest. Then we can er — well — daddle them!

Dame Daddle 'em? What on earth are you on about? We're not hanging around here daddling with a bunch of horrible hairy cutthroats! We're getting out of it — Pronto!

Jim But what about all the rent money he owes you?

She considers momentarily

Dame Where's the key?

They yank the key from its string around Billy's neck and run upstairs

Blind Puke (*off*) Down with the door, lads!
Pirates (*off*) In! In! Ooof!

*The door collapses under a tangle of grimy bodies as Blind Puke, Israel
Feet, and half a dozen other disreputable looking characters with brightly
coloured handkerchiefs knotted around their heads, burst in downstairs*

Israel Feet (*getting up*) All right, Puke. Where is he then?
Blind Puke He's here somewhere, shipmates. Turn the place over! Out with
   his liver!
Pirates His liver! His liver!
Israel Feet (*after a pause*) I wouldn't want *his* liver.
Blind Puke Well ... Out with his *spleen* then! Har har har! Lay to all hands!

*The Pirates scramble into a frenetic search. Israel promptly stumbles over
Billy's body*

Israel Feet Here! He's here, Puke!
Blind Puke The key! The key!
Pirates The key! The key!
Israel Feet Gone!
Pirates (*aghast*) Gone!

*Meanwhile, upstairs, Jim and the Dame succeed in opening the sea chest. She
peers inside and grabs up a fat purse of coin. Jim seizes up an oilskin packet*

Dame Here we are! Here's the dosh.
Jim And here's the map! Ha! Daddled, I think!

   They flee from the house via the back stairs

Blind Puke The chest!
Pirates The chest!

*The villains surge upstairs, bursting into Billy's room a split second after Jim
and his mother have vacated it. Israel rummages in the chest, and comes up
empty-handed*

Israel Feet Empty!
Pirates (*wailing*) Empty!
Blind Puke The map! The map!
Pirates The map! The map!
Israel Feet All right! All right! Stop shouting, will you. (*He searches again*)
   By thunder! Bill's been overhauled already, lads. The map's gone!

Pirates The map's gone!
Blind Puke Shut up! It's that boy, drat him! He's got the map, sure as pickled
eggs. I should ha' wrung his scrawny neck when I held him in these two
hands! The map's close by though — I can smell it!

*The Pirates, most impressed by this display of extrasensory perception, stand
nudging one another and nodding*

Pirates Aaaaaah ...
Israel Feet (*stolidly*) Well, if old Puke smells it, it must be somewhere's
hereabouts.
Pirates (*agreeing*) Old Puke smells ... Puke smells so it does ... He smells,
does Puke ... (*etc.*)
Blind Puke Wait! What was that?

A feeble toot on a bugle is heard nearby

Israel Feet The signal! That's the revenue men! Quick, lads! Run!
Blind Puke Run? What do you mean "run", you yellow dogs! Find the map
— then run!
Israel Feet They've daddled us, lads. Let's get out of here!
Blind Puke No! Wait! Shiver me timbers! If I had eyes! Am I to lose my
share for you? No man runs!
Israel Feet Fair enough.

*Israel puts his finger to his lips to signal quiet to the others and they all attempt
to tiptoe out past Puke. Unfortunately, Groundbait drops his cutlass, causing
Puke to spin around*

The sound of horses' hooves approaching fast can now be heard

Blind Puke Lads ... Are ye there, lads ... Israel? George? Groundbait? Where
are ye, shipmates?

*The sound effect of an entire heavy cavalry regiment at the gallop can now
be heard growing louder and louder*

Blind Puke Lads? Lads? Wait ... Don't leave me, lads ... Not old Puke ... Not
your old mate Puke ... Don't leave me to ...

*He blunders out through the door, straight into the path of the oncoming
sound effect*

Black-out

(*Off*) Aaaarrrrggghhh!!!!

Squire Polperro's drawing-room

Polperro, Dr Liversausage, Jim and Dame crowd around a table, with Bodmin and Newquay in waiting

Liversausage But this is quite remarkable, Jim. Killed by a sound effect you say. In all me medical career, I've never heard the like ——
Polperro Oh do shut up, Liversausage. We've more pressing matters to discuss.
Dame Exactly. Like this here map for instance.
Polperro Oons, madam! How dare you intrude on a conversation between two gentlemen!
Dame Oh, well, fine. I'll just take the map and go, shall I? C'mon, Jim.
Polperro No! No! Wait! Let's not be too hasty, ha ha ...
Liversausage Come, Mrs Ladd, you know very well that our worthy Squire is sometimes a little — reckless with his words.
Dame What, you mean words like "guttersnipe" for instance? "Ill-bred"? "Flogged"? "Transported"?
Polperro Just a small misunderstanding, dear lady. Me only daughter, doncha know. Fella can't be too careful. Still, we know better now don't we. Brave lad, your Jim. (*Patting Jim's head*) Fine, upstanding young cove. Smart as paint, young Jim. Erm ...
Dame All right. That'll do. Apology accepted.
Polperro Apology! Hrrrrumph!
Liversausage (*holding up the map*) Do you know what this is, Jim?
Jim I believe it to be a map, sir, showing the whereabouts of treasure buried by the infamous pirate captain, Squint. (*To Polperro*) Do you mean to find it, sir?
Polperro I do indeed, Jim. And it so happens that I have a sloop fitted out and ready for just such a venture. She's lying in Bristol Docks, ready to take on hands. *The Grand Pianola* she's called, Jim, and a sweeter schooner never put to sea. I'd like you to join me, lad. It's the chance of a lifetime for a young shaver like you!
Dame Hang on! What about an old non-shaver like me. Where he goes — I go.

Polperro A woman at sea! No no. That would be most irregular ...
Dame That's the deal. Take it or leave it — or shall we take *our* map and go?
Polperro You could never find the treasure without my ship!
Dame And you could never find it without our map!
Polperro Ha!
Dame Ha!
Polperro (*knowing he is beaten*) S'Death! Oh very well ... But it's *my* expedition. All right?
Dame Fine.
Polperro I shall be admiral. You, Liversausage, are ship's doctor. Jim here — the cabin boy.
Dame Oooh! How excitin'! And what shall I be?
Polperro In the ruddy way I should imagine! (*Turning away*) Redruth!
Bodmin Bodmin, sir.
Polperro Whatever. Ask Miss Nancy to join us for a moment will you?
Bodmin (*bowing*) Sir.

Bodmin exits

Polperro Now then, on the subject of crew, I have already engaged a captain, a most trustworthy fellow — although somewhat sour of countenance.
Dame (*drily*) Perhaps he's been fed too much of your rhubarb.

Polperro regards her narrowly

Polperro (*continuing*) More importantly, I have found a ship's cook! A most engaging rascal. Would you believe, the fellow only has one leg!

Long, drawn out dramatic chord. Jim and the Dame gape at each other, then at the audience

Jim
Dame } (*together*) One leg!
Liversausage How sirrah! You've signed a one-legged man as cook?
Polperro Don't scoff me, dear fellow. The man's a perfect trump! If it weren't for Slither — Long John Slither he is called — I would never have found the rest of the crew. Do you know, he's assembled a company of some of the roughest, toughest old salts you could ever wish to crew a Man o' War!

Nancy rushes in, Bodmin flustering behind

Nancy Oh Jim!

Jim Nancy!

Nancy Jim. Is it true? Are you leaving me?

Jim Erm — well ...

Polperro He is indeed, my dear. We sail on the morning tide!

Nancy (*histrionically*) But you can't take him away from me! You can't!

Romantic music swells threateningly. Squire Polperro viciously chops it off with a swipe of his hand

Polperro I jolly well can actually! (*Hissing at her*) Why do you think I'm taking the grotty little ragamuffin with me at all?

Nancy Very well. (*Resolved*) I'm coming too.

Polperro You certainly are not! The high seas are no place for a young lady of quality.

Dame (*to the audience*) You notice *I'll* be all right though.

Nancy But, Father!

Polperro No! That's me last word on the subject. Now, the rest of you, come into me library. We have admiralty charts to examine, and a vessel to provision! (*To Nancy*) I'll speak to you later, my girl.

All exit except for Nancy

Nancy (*to the audience*) Ha! That's what he thinks! Well I shall go — I shall! (*She thinks*) Wait a moment — I have it! I'll disguise myself as a boy and join the ship as humble cabin lad. Then I'll be with my own sweet Jim — and part of the adventure to boot! Rat me! What times we shall have! What larks! Huzza!

Song 4 (Nancy)

Music finally swells unimpeded, allowing Nancy to sing — not the threatened romantic exposition, but a lively, upbeat number instead

At the end of the song, there is a Black-out

SCENE 5

The taproom of "The Spyglass Inn", Bristol Docks

The crew are all assembled. Long John Slither, Groundbait, Israel Feet, Merry, and many more. Pink Dog drinks alone in the corner

She slinks out as Jim enters

Jim Mr Slither?
Slither Such is my name. And whom do I have the honour of h'addressin'?
Jim Jim Ladd, Mr Slither. I have a message from Squire Polperro.
Slither Well, fire away, matey. You're amongst friends here.
Jim (*regarding the sprawled crew members dubiously*) The squire sends his
  compliments, Mr Slither, and begs you to ensure all hands are aboard by
  four this afternoon.
Slither All hands aboard by four ... Hear that, lads? Stand by to go about!
  Dooty is dooty, shipmates! Well, look lively, lads!

The crew grumble as they get up and finish their drinks

Jim Are they *all* sailing with us, Mr Slither?
Slither Indeed they are, lad, every last one o' them.
Jim And can they all be, well — trusted?
Slither Why bless me yes! Hear that, lads: boy's a-wonderin' if some o' you
  might not be scallywags!

The Pirates laugh mechanically

  Now Jim — I can call you Jim, can't I?

Jim nods

  These here lads may not be pretty, and they don't look much, but they been
  with me through some rare ol' times, Jim. And every last one o' them
  straight as a frigate's mast. Course, we all has our own weaknesses don't
  we, lad? Our little dodges to earn us a crust. An' if you'd let me, Jim, I'd
  be proud as Punch to show you how you may return from this voyage a
  gen'lman. That's if, you wuz to throw your hat in with me, o'course. Let
  me put it this way.

Song 5 (Slither and Pirates)

  (*Breathless and flushed after the song*) Well ... What do you say, Jim?
Jim I — I don't know. I'll think about what you've said. I'd better get back
  to the ship.

Jim exits hurriedly

Slither (*softly*) Make your mind up quickly, Jim Ladd, for you ain't got much
  thinkin' time left! Ha ha ha ha!

Israel Feet Bah! Why waste your breath, John? I say we acts now — slit the cub's gizzard and pitch his body into the drink.

Slither And I say there'll be no slittin' o' gizzards in here. Leastways, not till *I* says the word! Ha ha ha ha!

Nancy enters the bear pit. She is now disguised as a ship's boy, fetchingly attired in close fitting knee-breeches and a swashbuckling hero shirt. She is barefoot, her hair tucked up beneath a bright woollen cap, with a matching sash around her waist

Audience participation as she enters

Nancy (*very jaunty*) Save ye, gentlemen, save ye!
Slither Well now, what have we here?

The Pirates crowd around her, but she is far from intimidated

Nancy (*saluting*) Dick the cabin boy reporting for ship's duties, Mr Quartermaster sir!
Slither Is that so? Well, well ... Ain't you a sharp lad, to be sure. Two cabin boys. What an embarrassment of riches, eh lads? Well young Dick, put your paw there——

They shake hands

— and welcome aboard, shipmate. Here's to an eventful voyage, eh? Ha ha ha!
Pirates Ha ha ha!
Nancy (*entering into the spirit of things*) Ha ha ha!

The Pirates all stare at her in surprise. Black-out. Stirring seafaring music as the scene is changed

SCENE 6

The deck of "The Grand Pianola"

She is ready for sea, the entire company assembled

The Dame arrives, clambering over the side with a great deal of luggage and commotion. She has changed into an outrageous pantomime dame sailor outfit

Dame Coo-eee! Sorry I'm so late. I just had to slip into something more seaworthy!

Song 6 (Dame and Company)

Smellit (*to Squire Polperro*) Sir. If we're to catch the tide, we need to put to sea without further delay.
Liversausage Ah, Mrs Ladd. Allow me to introduce you to our captain, ma'am.
Dame Oooh, ta ever so!

Liversausage leads her up to Smellit

Ah yes! You must be Smelly.

All snigger, except Smellit, who remains stony faced

Smellit Smellit. *Cap'n* Smellit to you. (*To Polperro*) Who is this personage? I warn you, sir, I'll have no truck with strumpets nor women of easy virtue aboard my ship.
Dame Strumpets? Easy virtue? Ooh, how dare you!
Polperro (*apologetically*) I fear the lady must sail with us perforce, Captain.
Smellit Indeed, sir. Then be so kind as to keep her out of my way. I don't want to see her near my poop.
Dame Oooh! I don't want anything to do with your poop! You filthy little man!
Polperro (*hastily*) Well, Smellit, what do you think of her?
Smellit (*regarding the Dame*) In truth, sir, I find her downright plain, and at least four stones too heavy.
Polperro No, no, no ... Not her! I mean *The Grand Pianola*! All shipshape and seaworthy?
Smellit She's a trim enough barque, sir. I can't speak more nor that, not having seen her tried. For the rest, I don't like this cruise, I don't like the crew, and — (*looking at the Dame*) I don't like the passengers. And that's short and sweet.
Dame (*heavy irony*) Well, say what you mean, why don't you?
Smellit A voyage to hunt for buried treasure! Pah! I don't hold with it, sir! And what's more, there's already been too much blabbing!
Polperro Blabbing!

All look at the Dame

Dame (*protesting*) What! What!

Smellit However, sir, you'll find I do my duty. (*Shouting*) Stand by to cast off!

Polperro Death and fire, Liversausage! This is not to be borne! Feller's an intolerable humbug!

Bodmin and Newquay enter carrying the Squire's trunk between them. Both are incongruously garbed in bright yellow PVC sou'westers, storm capes and sea boots

Smellit (*turning back to Polperro*) One thing more, sir — there are too many landlubbers aboard for my liking.

Polperro Landlubbers! Are you referring to me, sir?

Smellit No, sir. I'm referring to them. (*He points at Bodmin and Newquay*) Who are they, sir?

Polperro Them? Why, they're me — um ... what's the word?

Newquay (*helpfully*) Footmen, sir?

Polperro Lackeys. (*Bawling at them*) Redruth!

Bodmin Bodmin, sir!

Polperro Don't answer back! Leave that. Get below and take that ridiculous gear off!

Bodmin Ay ay, Admiral! Right away, sir! (*He turns on Newquay*) See! I told you the admiral wouldn't like it, didn't I?

They exit, Bodmin belabouring Newquay with his sou'wester

Polperro (*shouting at Nancy*) You there! Ship's boy! Fetch me a flask o' French brandy from me trunk!

Nancy Ay ay, sir! (*She brings it to him, carefully averting her face*)

Polperro Much obliged. Here's to success, eh Liversausage! (*Peering at Nancy*) I say! Don't I know you?

Nancy No, sir. Don't think so, sir, begging your worship's pardon, sir.

Polperro No? Oh, All right. Well, cut along. (*Turning to Smellit*) Whenever you're ready, Cap'n.

Nancy scuttles away as the ship's company prepare to put to sea

Smellit Ay ay, sir. Slip the forr'ad cable, Mr Mate.

Israel Feet (*bellowing*) Slip cable forr'ad!

Smellit And aft.

Israel Feet (*bellowing*) Slip the cable, aft!

Voice Cables away, Mr Mate!

Israel Feet Cables away, Cap'n.

Smellit All right. Heave up the anchor, Mr Mate.

Israel Feet Ay ay, sir. Weigh anchor!
Merry Right, me buckos, put your shoulders to it! Heave!

The capstan grinds around one notch

  And again. Heave!

Bang on cue, Nancy is sick over the upstage rail

Groundbait Now Barbecue! Tip us a stave! The old one!
Slither Ay ay, mates! (*He sings*)
                        Fifteen men on a dead man's chest!
Crew (*heaving*) Yo ho *ho*! And a bottle of rum!
Slither   Drink and the Devil had done for the rest!
Crew (*heaving*) Yo ho *ho*! And a bottle of rum!

The song continues throughout the following dialogue

Smellit Make all sail, Bosun.
Merry Ay ay, Cap'n. Make sail, you dogs. Make sail!
Smellit Loose off the tops'ls.
Merry Loose the tops'ls!
Voice Tops'ls away, sir!

Sound effects of sails flapping and starting to fill with wind

Smellit Sheet home the T'gallants.
Merry Sheet 'em home aloft!
Voice Sheet 'em home!
Dame (*conversationally to Smellit*) I've got a duvet at home — not sheets.
  Much warmer ...
Israel Feet (*to the capstan crew*) Heave away, lads. Yarely now.
Dame Oh yes. Go on, lads. Yarely.
Smellit Stretch her luff, Mr Bosun.
Merry Stretch her luff!
Dame Stretch her ... (*Hitting Merry*) Oh, you rude man!
Smellit Haul taut!
Merry Ay ay, sir! Haul taut!
Dame (*getting into the swing of things*) Haul taut! Haul taut, everybody!
Smellit (*angry*) Belay that talk!
Merry Belay that talk!
Dame Belay that talk!
Smellit (*furious*) Stow it, I say!

Merry Stow it!

Dame (*to the crew*) You'd better stow it. 'Cos he's getting cross.

Smellit (*roaring*) Madam, if you don't cease your infernal row, I'll have you thrown in the brig, by thunder!

Dame Well! (*Huffily*) There's no need to be like that. I was just entering into the spirit of things.

Smellit Watch your spanker, Mr Mate.

Dame Spanker? Oooh! The man's a pervert!

Smellit Steady as she goes, helmsman — bring her into the wind.

Dame Oh, I think I've been brung into the wind already. (*She emits a monstrous burp*) Oh! S'cuse me! (*Proffering a jar*) Pickled egg anybody?

Nancy who has just begun to feel better, takes one look, and rushes to the rail again

Israel Feet Anchor's weighed, Cap'n!

Dame Ten stone six!

Smellit (*ignoring her*) Thank you, Mr Mate. Stand her down for the open sea. We'll run before the wind!

Dame (*mumbling*) I wish I could.

Israel Feet Ay ay, sir!

Smellit Seaward ho, Mr Mate!

Israel Feet Seaward ho, Cap'n!

All Seaward ho! Huzza!

Music as the entire company surge backwards and forwards across the deck, as if beset by a sudden swell, leading into:

Song 7 (All)

The Lights fade to Black-out. There is a sudden outbreak of sound effects: seagulls crying, cordage creaking, timbers groaning, waves slooshing, so on and so forth. Atmospheric, in a manner o' speakin'

SCENE 7

The same. Four weeks later

Jim and the Dame are taking the sea air

Dame Well, Jim ... Here we are, all at sea. Four weeks, and never a sign of land. Not been an overly eventful passage, has it?

Jim Apart from four members of the crew mysteriously lost overboard.

Dame Ah yes ... The four members of the crew *not* signed on by your chum Long John Slither you mean?

Jim (*uncomfortably*) Er — yes.

Dame Yes. And you don't find that just the teensy-weensiest little bit suspicious?

Jim Well ...

Dame I tell you what I think, young feller me lad, I think that one-legged imposter and his good-for-nothin' cronies are a bunch of constipators.

Jim You mean conspirators.

Dame I know what I mean. And speak of the devil ...

Long John Slither enters, studiously ignoring any audience participation

Slither Avast behind!

Dame You're too late, we've already done that one.

Slither Ah ... Now I gets the feelin' that you don't like me overmuch.

Dame Always trust your feelings, that's what my old mum used to say.

Slither 'Tis a great shame, so it is — for you and I could get along famously.

Dame Oh yus?

Slither Ay. Do you know *why* they calls me Long John?

Dame I shudder to think!

Slither Well then — I could splice your mainbrace, belike ...

Dame I could put you in a neck brace, belike.

Slither Ha ha! How would you like to be caught amidships?

Dame How would you like a kick in the crutch?

Slither (*holding on to his crutch, suddenly uncertain*) You never would ...

Dame I wasn't talking about that.

Slither (*changing tack*) Here now! Have you seen Cap'n Haddock? I been lookin' all over for the dratted bird.

Jim Cap'n Haddock, Mr Slither?

Slither My parrot, lad — Cap'n Haddock I calls him. Tell 'ee what, why don't you help me look for him?

Jim Sure.

Long John Slither and Jim go off

The Dame is left alone on deck. She wanders down to talk to the audience

Dame Parrot indeed! What a load of nonsense! Whoever heard of a parrot on a boat like this? *Pirate*, yes, that I could believe, but parrot ...? I mean honestly — have you seen a parrot?

*Needless to say, this is precisely the moment at which a giant, crimson
pantomime parrot ambles on and crosses to perch behind the Dame*

You have? Where? What, behind me? Nar ... You're fibbing, aren't you?
Shall I have a look?

*And so on. Traditional business, as practised by all self-respecting panto-
mime animals, until finally the Dame and Cap'n Haddock come face to beak*

Eeeek!

Long John Slither and Jim return

Slither Why, and here he is! Top o' the mornin' t'ye, Cap'n! Let's have a
bit of a yarn, eh?

Dame (*gobsmacked*) Bloomin' heck! What a whoppin' great enormous bird.

Slither Aaar ... Still, I daresay folks say the same about you, ma'am.

Dame Watch it, Tosh.

Slither Fact is, he's a Guatemalan crimson parakeet is the cap'n, and his tribe
don't come no bigger nor that. He's three hundred year old this parrot, like
as not. They lives forever mostly.

Dame I know how he feels — he should try sitting through this pantomime.

Cap'n Haddock (*suddenly flapping his wings*) Pieces of seven! Pieces of
seven!

Dame 'Ere! Aren't parrots s'posed to say "pieces of eight"?

Slither Oh ay. But the cap'n here ain't too bright. He can only count as far
as seven.

Cap'n Haddock Long John's a thieving git! Long John's a thieving git!
Aaark!

Dame What did he say?

Slither Nothing, ha ha. He just says the first thing as comes into his head.

Cap'n Haddock Crooked as a fourpenny bit! Aaark!

Dame He says you're crooked as a fourpenny bit.

Cap'n Haddock Thick as clotted cream! Aaark!

Dame He says you're thick as ——

Slither I heard him. Don't you mind the cap'n, he's just sore 'cos I won't let
him perch on my shoulder now 'e's growed so big.

Dame Why not?

Slither 'Cos there's only one poop deck aboard this ship, (*tapping his
shoulder*) and this ain't it.

Dame Go on, Cap'n, say something else.

Cap'n Haddock (*to Jim*) Who's a pretty boy then?

Slither Aaar. That's more like it, Cap'n.

Cap'n Haddock (*to Slither*) Thieving git!
Slither Right, come here, you ——
Cap'n Haddock Stand by to repel boarders! Aaaark!

Slither grabs the parrot around the throat. The parrot siezes Long John's nose in its beak. They tussle

Slither All right! All right! You can have a lump o' sugar! Just get off me!

The parrot releases his nose, and turns to peer interestedly at the Dame

Cap'n Haddock (*to the Dame*) Who's a repulsive old boot then? Aaark!
Dame Cheek!
Slither Right, come along, Cap'n. Give me half a moment, Jim, then you come down the galley and help me peel some spuds, eh? I can't find young Dick nowhere — seems a mite workshy that one.
Cap'n Haddock Lovely bum though! Aaark!
Slither I'm getting seriously worried about you ...

He goes off with the parrot

Jim See— Long John's a splendid fellow really. A very different creature from the likes of Blind Puke and Pink Dog.
Dame Yes, well ... I'm not so sure — I fancy there's more to Mr Slither than meets the eye.

Nancy saunters on, attempting to look convincingly seamanlike by puffing nonchalantly on a clay pipe

Oho! Look who's crawled out of the woodwork now there's no jobs to be done. The ship's cook was looking for you.
Nancy Really?
Dame Really.
Nancy (*shrugging*) Hey-ho!
Dame Tell me, young Dick, what I want to know, is why have we got *two* cabin boys aboard this floating bathtub, eh?
Nancy I'm sure I couldn't tell you.
Dame Oh I'm sure you could. You see, I don't think half the people on board this ship are who they say they are — including you.
Nancy (*innocently*) No?
Dame No. Still, none of my business, is it. Just duck into the barrel and fetch me an apple would you, there's a good lad.

Nancy Ay ay, ma'am. (*Peering into the barrel*) Oh! There's only one left. Right at the bottom. (*She reaches down to the bottom of the barrel, so that the upper part of her body disappears inside*) I can't quite reach it.
Dame Never mind.

The Dame grabs Nancy by the ankles, upending her into the barrel. Nancy yelps and flails her legs in mid-air

Nancy Help! What are you doing?
Dame I'm going to ask you a few easy-peasy questions — only I don't want to hear no porky pies this time.
Nancy Let me go!
Dame Feather, Jim.
Jim Er — feather.

Jim goes off

Cap'n Haddock (*off*) Aaaark!

Jim wanders back on clutching a large crimson feather

Jim (*handing it over*) Feather.
Nancy Oh no. Please don't ...
Dame Now then. Who are you — really?
Nancy I've told you! I'm Dick the cabin boy.
Dame All right. Have it your own way. (*To the audience*) Shall I?

Pantomime audiences, being essentially vindictive in nature, may be expected to shout "yes". If not — improvise. Either way, the Dame imprisons Nancy's bare feet under one arm and remorselessly applies the feather

Nancy No! No! Please! Stop! All right! All right! I'll tell you!
Dame Aha! Who are you then?
Nancy It's me! Nancy!
Dame (*amazed*) Nancy!
Jim (*rushing to the barrel*) Nancy!
Nancy Oh Jim!
Jim (*plunging his head down into the barrel*) Oh Nancy!

Music begins to swell romantically again — rather inappropriately given that both parties are now head down in a barrel

Dame Oh no! Look who's coming back!

The music stops dead as the Dame releases Nancy's legs, allowing her to slide completely down into the apple barrel. Jim pops up

It's Slither! Coming this way! Quick, Jim! Scarper!

Jim But what about Nancy?

Dame (*looking at her empty hands*) Ooops! Butterfingers! Keep your noddle down, Nance. If the crew find out you're the squire's daughter, you'll really be for it!

Jim But shouldn't we tell the squire she's here?

Dame Get off! He'd go ballistic! And you know who he'd blame, don't you?

Jim I can guess.

Dame Right. Come on then!

The Dame and Jim rush upstage, flinging themselves into hiding behind the quarter deck, L

Slither, Israel, and Groundbait O' Flaherty enter R, *crossing to drop to the floor around the poop*

Slither So we're agreed then, lads. The moment we make land, we cut 'em down — like so much pork. Squire, Doctor, Cap'n — the lot.

The barrel starts to sidle surreptitiously off

Israel Ay ay, John. That's the ticket! When the time comes — why let her rip! And we'll make that scurvy boy and the potty old battleship walk the plank, eh?

Dame (sotto voce *to Jim*) What potty old battleship?

Slither Good idea. Just for a lark, eh? Then we'll have the ship, the map — and Squint's treasure to roll in! Ha ha ha ha! We'll live like kings, by the powers!

Audience participation

Aaar, stow your noise, ye maggots! You lot are more creepy than a tribe o' weevils in a barrel load o' ship's biscuit!

Audience participation

An' speakin' o' barrels — Groundbait, fetch me an apple from yonder tub, there's a good lad. To wet me pipe like.

The barrel comes scuttling back into its original position

Groundbait (*without looking*) Barrel's empty, John.

Slither (*banging it with his crutch*) That ain't empty! Root about in the bottom, lad. You'll come up wi' summat sweet and juicy, and you may lay to that!

Dame (*aside*) How right you are.

Slither Oh, never mind! I'll do it. (*To the audience*) I'll take a peep meself shall I, shipmates?

Audience participation

No? No? And why not in blazes? What have you lot got to hide from Old John Slither?

He goes to reach into the barrel. An apple flies up into the air. Slither catches it in surprise and regards it quizzically

Well sink me! Now I calls that mighty pecooliar. (*He tugs a huge flintlock pistol from his belt*) I think I need to take a closer squint at this here barrel.

Just in the nick of time, there is a shout from aloft

Voice Land ho! Land ho!

Israel Feet Land! Land, John! 'Tis Treasure Island for sure.

Slither (*smiling broadly, the apple barrel forgotten*) Oh ay, Israel, couldn't be no other in these waters.

The rest of the crew flood on to the deck, The Captain, Squire and Doctor making straight for the quarter deck. As all the crew run to look from the far rail, Nancy clambers from the apple barrel and runs off

Squire Well! There she is, Liversausage! What did I tell you?

Liversausage We're not out of the woods yet.

Jim Doctor! I have to talk to you and the other gentlemen, sir. A most urgent matter.

Liversausage Very well, Jim. Join us below in the captain's cabin in one minute. (*He whispers to Polperro and Smellit*)

Polperro and Smellit exit immediately, Bodmin and Newquay trailing behind. Jim and the Dame wander off the opposite direction, whistling with exaggerated innocence

Israel Feet (*watching them go*) Well, John? Do we do it now, by thunder?

Slither When I gives the word, Israel, and not before. George, fetch a cask of grog, I think this calls for a celebration. Here's to Cap'n Squint, eh lads? May he rot in hell! Ha ha ha!

As he takes a savage bite out of the apple, the Lights fade to Black-out

SCENE 8

Captain Smellit's cabin

The Lights come up on Jim and the Dame who have just finished relating the bad news to Smellit, Polperro, Liversausage, Newquay and Bodmin

Polperro Oons, sirrah! The damnable scoundrels ... And to think they're Englishmen! (*He is struck by a sudden thought*) Split me! You don't imagine they're actually a pack of Frenchies, do you!
Liversausage (*ignoring Polperro*) The entire crew you say, Jim? Every last man?
Jim I'm afraid so, Doctor.
Liversausage Whilst we number just four.
Dame Oi!
Liversausage Five.

Bodmin clears his throat politely

Polperro Oh, and not forgetting Redruth and thingummy here ——
Bodmin Bodmin, sir.
Polperro Ah yes, Redruth and Bodmin.
Bodmin No, sir, it's Bodmin and ——
Dame Oh what does it matter what their names are, they're both completely useless anyway.
Newquay Here — hang on a minute.
Polperro (*regretfully*) Yes, there is that.
Bodmin Oh thanks.
Doctor Now what about young Dick, the cabin boy?
Polperro Despicable rascal — comes from a bad family, it's written all over him.
Dame Oh, you're right there — I know the father quite well. The man's a complete fruitbat.
Polperro Really?

Dame Oh yes. Total crackpot — a galloping wazzock. But you can take it from me, we can definitely trust the er — boy. Jim's abnormally fond of him — isn't that right, Jim?

Jim Um — yes.

Liversausage Eight then. Against how many?

Smellit (*consulting the ship's log*) Forty-six.

Polperro (*breezily*) Oh. Not bad odds then.

Dame Shut up. What are we going to do about it, that's what I want to know?

Smellit Gentlemen, there is only one sound course of action. The mutineers will not act until we are all ashore and in the open. I propose we land a boat, well provisioned with salt pork, muskets, and powder — under the pretence of carrying out a reconnaisance, d'ye see. We locate the treasure, recover it, and then occupy the old stockade shown on the map, before the villains have even set foot on the island! From our stronghold, we can pick 'em off at our leisure.

Polperro Oh jolly good! First rate, Smellit!

Dame (*unimpressed*) Stonkin' ...

Liversausage There's only one thing amiss with your plan, Captain.

Smellit Indeed, sir?

Liversausage The ship's boat can only carry six.

Polperro Ah.

Dame (*without compunction*) All right, so we leave Dick.

Smellit And one other.

Dame What you all looking at me for? No! Absolutely not! I'm not staying on this floatin' coffin with a horde of desperate bandits for company.

Jim (*nobly*) It's all right, Mother, I'll stay. I'll, er — (*winking at the audience*) see to young Dick.

Dame Oh no you won't, my lad! I'll stay meself. Don't worry, *I'll* take care of young Dick!

Polperro (*moved*) Noble sacrifice! 'Pon my soul — I've misjudged you, Mrs Ladd. I had you down as a grasping, cowardly, scheming old trollop.

Dame How nice of you to say so, Squire. (*To the audience*) He's goin' to have to go.

Polperro But now I perceive that we have much to be grateful for.

Dame (*under her breath*) Yes, and you more than most. If only you knew ...

Smellit Gentlemen. To the jolly boat!

Music. The Lights fade to Black-out

Scene 9

The deck of "The Grand Pianola"

The Lights come up on the deck. Apparently, one of the ship's boats containing the Squire's party (out of view) has just been lowered over the side. As they row smartly away from The Grand Pianola, *the Dame is shouting after them and waving a grubby handkerchief*

Dame Well, bye then. Got your packed lunch, Jim? ... Eh? ... Oh no, don't you worry about me, I'll be right as rain. ... What's that? ... No, no, Squire, I'm sure the beady-eyed Frenchies won't do anything hasty. (*She turns around*)

The Pirates are drawn up in a solid troop, dripping menace, bristling with weapons, and all glaring at her

Er — was there somethin'?
Slither Yes. This here vessel is under new management. *Cap'n* Slither at your service, mum.
Dame Oh ... Now that's what I call career progression: chief cook and bottle washer one minute, ship's captain the next! (*Pointing*) Ooooh I say! Look over there!

She points behind them. As they all turn to look, she makes a run for it

She disappears down the companionway to the foc'sle — but promptly retreats back on, followed by a menacing, pink clad figure (Pink Dog) wielding a wicked-looking cutlass

(*Apalled*) Pink Dog!
Pink Dog The very same!
Dame You don't mean you've been stowed away in the foc'sle the whole bloomin' voyage. Not with — not with all those — all those horrible, sweaty sailors!
Pink Dog That's right.
Dame Oooh, you lucky moo! What was it like?
Slither Belay that talk! You, my pretty, has somethin' I want.
Dame I know, and I've already told you — you're not havin' it!
Slither The map.
Dame (*relieved*) Oh that! Oh no, I haven't got that.
Slither *What?*
Dame I handed it over to old Polperro as soon as we sailed out of Bristol Docks.

Slither *What?*

Dame Couldn't make head nor tail of it to tell you the truth.

Slither Then you and me is goin' to sit down, have a good long yarn, an' see if we can't remember all the little details. (*Shouting*) Like where the blessed treasure's sittyated!

Dame Ha! Bilge water to that!

Slither Groundbait. Run out a plank. We're going to have us a walkin'.

The Pirates cheer

Dame Wait a minute. It's starting to come back to me ...

George Merry enters, dragging Nancy by one arm

Merry John! Look who I found a-skulkin' in the mizzen.

Slither Well, well ... If it t'ain't young Dick, the ship's lad. Now look 'ee, young spark, you've seen the score I reckon. What d'ye say — are ye with us, or agin us?

Nancy Cap'n Slither sir, I have only one thing to say to you. And that is that you are a murdering, treacherous, thorough-going scoundrel! You'd look remarkable fine, sir, swinging from that yard-arm!

Slither I'll take that as a no, shall I?

Nancy Join your crew of scurvy renegades, sir? I'd rather die in a dirty ditch!

Slither That can be arranged. Israel! Clap him in irons and pitch him in the scuppers. He'll make a dandy sight, blindfolded and dancing a hornpipe on a plank's end. Ha ha ha!

Audience participation

Nancy Take your hands off me you filthy, mutinous, black-hearted vermin!

In the tussle her hat falls off, revealing her lustrous locks. The Pirates step back, gawping in surprise

Israel Feet By all the powers! 'Tis a wench!

Slither So I see, shipmates. But who? That's what I want to know ...

Pink Dog What's it matter who she is? I say, she still walks the plank! Eh, lads?

Cheers of approval from the rest of the Pirates. Chants of "Plank, Plank, Plank"

Slither (*hastily*) Oh ay. She'll take the long drop right enough. But my curiosity's been pricked just the same.

Nancy I'll tell you exactly who I am, you shabby, backsliding mountebank! I'm ——

Dame (*quickly interrupting*) She's my Jim's bit of fluff, that's who.

Slither His bit o' fluff?

Dame And why not? (*Nodding at Pink Dog*) You brought your doxy along, didn't you?

Pink Dog Why, you ——

Slither Lay off, I say!

Pink Dog (*viciously*) Let me flog her, Cap'n.

Slither You won't get much for her — she's well past her sell-by date. (*Boom Boom!*)

All the Pirates laugh uproariously and for far too long at Long John's joke

(*Snarling*) All right. That's enough. Throw the wench in the brig.

Nancy is dragged off, bawling most unladylike curses and imprecations at her gaolers

(*Turning back to the Dame*) Now, you and I are going to have that little chat. But first, tell me, Mr Bosun, how far has that blessed bum-boat got?

Merry (*looking through a telescope*) Halfway to the beach, Long John.

Slither Then that's far enough, I fancy. Israel, run out the gun.

Israel Feet (*grinning*) Ay ay, Cap'n Slither!

Dame No. You wouldn't!

Slither And Mr O'Flaherty.

Groundbait Ay, Skipper?

Slither Run up the Jolly Roger!

Groundbait Ay ay, sir!

Dire and portentous music as that black and infamous rag is scurried up the mainstays. The Lights cross-fade downstage to the Squire's party in the longboat. Bodmin and Newquay are toiling at the oars, Smellit and Liversausage are in the stern, Jim and Squire Polperro in the bows

Jim Um ... shouldn't we row a bit faster, sir? In case the mutineers rumble us.

Polperro No. Damnable rascals are probably getting blotto on a pipe of me choice Madeira even as we speak. In any event, we're well out of musket range. No, have no fear, young Jim, we're in absolutely no danger out here. Nothing's going to happ ——

There is an enormous, ear-splitting bang, followed by the deafening scream of a flying cannon ball, and a great splash next to the longboat — rocking it, and nearly spilling its occupants

Liversausage You were saying?

Jim (*pointing back to the ship*) Look, sir! They've hoisted the skull and crossbones!

Smellit The game's afoot then! Pull for the beach, men, cheerily now!

Bodmin (*starting to crack*) What do you mean cheerily? There's some ruddy maniac lobbing dirty great cannon balls at us! We're not out for a leisurely scull round the village pond, you know!

Polperro Redruth!

Bodmin And another thing! Don't keep calling it a jolly boat! It's not jolly — it's flamin' dismal.

Polperro (*shouting*) Redruth!

Bodmin (*snivelling*) Bodmin, sir.

Polperro Quite so. Now pull yourself together, sirrah, and remember you're an Englishman — not one of those detestable frog-eaters.

Liversausage Rot me, Polperro, but you're becoming tiresome! They are *not* Frenchmen, just a bunch of common or garden British scumbags! The sort you meet on any package holiday.

Smellit In heaven's name, gentlemen! Put up and row!

The Lights cross-fade once more to the deck of The Grand Pianola, *where the Dame is furiously berating Long John Slither*

Dame Oi! You must be a banana short of a bunch, pal! I just told you that he's got the ruddy map! Fat lot of good it's going to be to any of us at the bottom of the bay! What are you trying to sink them for?

Slither Oh, I ain't tryin' to sink 'em — just keepin' 'em abreast o' developments, in a manner o' speakin'. If I'd wanted to sink 'em, I'd ha' let fly a full broadside by thunder! That there was just a little summat down on account — to ginger 'em up a touch. Ha ha ha!

Dame (*coldly*) You really enjoy your work, don't you?

Slither Ah well, 'tis a fine thing to be a Gennelman o' Fortune, and you may lay to that. Now then, you and I is goin' to adjourn to the cap'n's stateroom to chew the fat — whiles Israel here goes to find a nice sturdy plank. Ha ha ha!

Music as the Lights cross-fade to the jolly boat which is now run up on the beach. The occupants struggle to unload muskets and casks of provisions

An ecstasy of sound effects may now erupt, as tropical waves lap the golden shore, coconuts drop from palm trees, and cicadas chirrup in the mangrove swamp. High in the rain forest canopy monkeys chatter, exotic birds shriek ... etc., etc. You get the picture

Polperro Splendid effort, chaps. Awfully well done. We made it. Er — now what?

Smellit Well, one thing's certain, there's no going back now — so we must go on. I fancy we shall not have long to wait before they mount a pursuit. Let us find the stockade. The map, sir, if you please.

Polperro Ah yes. Liversausage — the map.

Liversausage I haven't got it. I thought you had it.

Smellit Well, sir?

Polperro (*blanching*) Oh God. She's still got it.

Smellit What? Not that confounded woman?!

Liversausage Death and fire, Polperro! You left the map on board! Then we must earnestly hope that the villains do not effect a bodily search of her person.

Polperro (*shuddering*) Let us hope not, sir — for their sakes.

Smellit I suggest we split into two groups and attempt to locate the stockade. The first party to find it, shall discharge a musket shot to summon the others. Are we agreed, gentlemen?

All Agreed.

Polperro Right then. Come, Liversausage, you, I, and the captain shall take the shore path, whilst Jim, Redruth, and wossisname, strike into the interior. All right, young Jim?

Jim Yes, sir.

Liversausage What's amiss, lad?

Jim I am worried, sir, for young Dick — and Mother.

Polperro Bravely now, lad. She can look after herself, you know.

Liversausage A formidable woman your mother, Jim.

Smellit The blaggards won't know what's hit 'em. Take my word for it.

Bodmin Serves them right, that's what I say. (*He nudges Newquay*)

Newquay What? Oh yes. They've really got it coming to them.

Jim Oh I say! Do you really think so?

All Oh yes.

Behind Jim's back they shake their heads and exchange knowing glances of doom and despondency

Polperro Now just remember, Jim. Above all, we are Englishmen! We'll get the better of this rag-bag gang of pestilent Frenchies! Just you wait and see. All is not lost.

Bodmin Just the map.
Polperro Yes. Just the map.
All Huzza!

Song 8 (All)

*Which concludes the first half d'ye see, and leads nicely into an interval —
and you may lay to that*

CURTAIN

ENTR'ACTE

ACT II

SCENE 1

Overture

The deck of "The Grand Pianola"

A sturdy plank has been lashed to the gunwales, jutting out over the sea. The Pirates are crowded on deck, an excited air of expectation about them. Nancy kneels to one side, already blindfolded and tied, in readiness for the pirates' macabre cabaret

The Dame is ushered on by Israel Feet

Dame (*protesting*) Look! I don't see what your problem is. I've told you where the treasure is buried, haven't I?

Slither Ah yes, let me see. (*He consults his notes, then in a whining voice:*) "In the *sand*."

Dame Well, I can't remember, can I. Look, you're making a terrible mistake, I tell you — I can't even swim.

Israel Feet So much the better. We won't have to lash no lead weights to your ankles then, will we?

Slither Blindfold, George.

Dame Why? What's he seen?

Merry steps forward with a length of soiled sailcloth

Hup! No need for that. (*Nobly*) Never forget that I am a Ladd.

Slither No ... Well, I don't think anyone's really fooled are they?

Dame Anyway, if I'm for the early bath, then I want to see the sun in the sky — the wind in the trees. Saturday's episode of *Brookside* ——

Slither Belay that! Any last requests?

Dame Yes. Drop dead.

Slither Sorry, can't oblige. On to the plank with her, me hearties!

Pirates The plank! The plank!

Dame All right! All right! No need to push! What's the big hurry!

Song 9 (Slither and Pirates)

During which the Dame is bundled unceremoniously on to the plank, edging gingerly along its entire length, until she reaches the end

Dame Now what?
Slither (*patiently*) You're *s'posed* to fall off.
Dame What — down there?
Slither That's it.
Dame Into the water?
Slither Yup.
Dame But I'll get wet.
Slither Hard tack!
Dame Shan't!
Slither (*getting bored*) All right, Groundbait, shoot her.

Groundbait steps forward with an evil grin and a large blunderbuss

Dame All right! All right! I'm going. Don't get yer pigtail in a pandemonium. Blimey! Now I know how a lemming feels ... BANZAI!

She jumps off the plank, plummetting with a cry, and disappearing from view. There is a tremendous splash from below, followed by an ominous glugging sound

Slither Blob overboard! Ha ha ha! Well, she made a big splash in the end! Next!

Audience participation as Nancy is hustled forward

Well now, my pretty. Anything to say, afore ye join the old trout in the pond?
Nancy (*very businesslike, despite her predicament*) Now look 'ee, Master Peg-Leg, you've had your fun — and to admiration, by thunder. But this has gone far enough, d'ye see? Now then, here it is: you and your picaroons clap yourselves in irons, turn the ship over to me, and I undertake to put in a good word for ye — before they hang you from the gibbet at Wapping Dock. How's that?
Slither Well! I calls that right handsome of ye, ma'am. Let me put it to Ship's Council. (*Turning to the pirates*) What d'ye say, lads?

An extremely loud bleep drowns out the Pirates' reply, which sounds suspiciously like:

Pirates B******s!
Slither Ah dear ... It seems I must regretfully decline your generous terms,
ma'am. (*Roaring*) On to the plank with her!
Pirates (*chanting*) Plank! Plank! Plank! Plank!

They cheer loudly as Nancy is manhandled roughly up on to the plank

Nancy Unhand me, you ungrateful scoundrels! Dammit all! I can't see
where I'm going!
Slither That's the general idea. Give her a prod.

*Pink Dog gives Nancy an enthusiastic poke with a cutlass point, forcing her
out along the plank*

Nancy Rat me! To think it's come to this. And all for love. Devil take ye, Jim
Ladd! Where were you when I needed you?

*The Dame, now a fearsome, seaweed covered apparition, suddenly
whooshes up from the surface*

Dame He's not here — but Mummy is!
Pirates (*falling back in terror*) Aaaaarggh! 'Tis a ghost! A ghost!
Dame Jump, Nancy! Jump!
Nancy But I'll drown!
Dame No you won't! (*She stands up*) It's only six inches deep!
Slither What?
Israel Feet We're aground! We've hit a sandbank, by thunder!
Slither What?
Merry (*looking over the far rail*) 'Tis true, John! She's fouled her bottom!
Nancy (*outraged*) I certainly have not!

*All the Pirates rush to the far rail, to find that whilst they've been occupied
with the spectacle of walking the plank to the seaward, The Grand Pianola
has indeed drifted aground, on to the barely submerged sands of the island*

Dame (*shouting*) Jump! You silly moo!
Slither (*bellowing*) Get her!

*The Pirates all make a rush for the near rail. Nancy jumps. There is another
splash as she lands, but she is immediately on her feet — revealing that the
ship is indeed lying in only six inches of water! The Dame whips Nancy's
blindfold off*

Dame Right! Run for it!

They leap out of the sea to flee out through the audience

The Pirates fire off a thundering volley of musket shots — all miss

Slither (*raging*) Avast, ye mealy swabs! Ye've let them get away! After
   them by thunder! Go! Go!

The Pirates swarm off, surging out through the audience in hot pursuit

Slither clumps down to address the audience

   I fancy you suppose they've got one over on me, do you? Eh? Well they
   haven't, and you may lay to that!

Audience participation

   Oh no they haven't!

Audience participation

   Aaar! Lay aft, ye noisome bilge-rats! Ye'll soon see the vengeance of
   Cap'n Slither by thunder! There's never a man as looked me between the
   eyes, and lived to see a good day afterwards! Them as dies will be the lucky
   ones! Ha ha ha ha!

   Slither stumps off cackling, oblivious to the jeers of the audience

The Lights fade to Black-out

*A musical chase sequence through the audience may now ensue if it proves
necessary to cover the change of scene*

SCENE 2

A stockade ashore

The Lights come up on the outer palisade of the stockade

*Polperro, Liversausage and Smellit approach a gate in the fence — which
appears unaccountably to be locked*

Polperro Here we are. (*Trying the handle*) 'Pon my sam! The dratted thing's locked!

Liversausage Locked? It can't be — this is a desert island, isn't it?

Don Iguana (*off*) *H*allo! Who ees eet?

A dark, moustachioed face appears over the palisade. It is Don Iguana Del Anaconda Con Queso

Polperro (*trying to sweep his sword out, but getting it embarrassingly entangled*) Frenchies! Frenchies — Devil take 'em!

Don Iguana Hey! Who are you calling Frenchy? Eengleesh peeg! There is only one theeng worse than a Gringo heretic like you, and that's a feelthy, snail-eating Froggy, comprendo?

Polperro Split me! He's a rascally Don!

Liversausage A Spaniard!

Don Iguana Bang on, camarado!

Polperro Well what's the blighter doing in our stockade? (*Calling up*) Who the devil are you, sirrah?

Don Iguana You have the very conseederable honour of addressing His Excellency, Don Iguana Del Anaconda Con Queso, Ambassador to Guadeloupe, by the grace of God and Hees Most Catholeec Majesty, Alfonso, King of España. Oy!

Polperro But hang it all — this is a British Island!

Don Iguana Not any more compadré! Now push off back to your sheep, before I *h*order my garrison to *h*open fire!

Polperro What garrison?

Don Iguana That's exactly what I said to Hees Most Catholeec Majesty, Alfonso, King of España. Oy!

Polperro There is no garrison!

Don Iguana That's exactly what Alfonso, King of España, said to me!

Polperro (*turning away to confer*) Feller's completely doolally, Liversausage! Mad as a dog. Can't we just shoot him?

Smellit I must counsel caution, sir. We wouldn't want a diplomatic incident on our hands.

Polperro But he's in our blessed stockade! And the blasted Frenchies will be here any minute!

Don Iguana Now push off, crazee Eengleesh privateer! Beefore you make-a me lose my temper.

Polperro Now hark 'ee, you daft Spanish onion, I'm not a privateer, I'm an English gentleman d'ye see!

Don Iguana Ha! So the Eengleesh Milord theenks he can outweet the cunning Spanish Señor does he? Theenk again, enchillada-face!

Polperro Right! That does it! We shall take the stockade by main force. Look to your weapons, gentlemen. Remember Cadiz!

Don Iguana Take one step closer, muchachos, and I shall give to you the full cannonado!

Polperro Oh come off it! You're never going to tell me you've got an artillery piece in there!

Don Iguana No. But I gotta plenty coconuts! (*He hurls a few hairy projectiles at Polperro*)

Polperro Garzoon! The feller's insufferable! I've had just about enough of this! Right. Up lads, and at 'em!

There is a sudden frantic strumming of Spanish guitars, and a sultry rattle of castanets

Donna Estella, a startlingly sumptuous figure in scarlet satin, suddenly appears beside the vacuously drooling Don Iguana, her shining black hair cascading in ringlets across her slender shoulders and on to the frilly white lacy bits that surround her ample ... Well, you get the picture

Donna Estella (*imperiously*) H-Wait!

Polperro (*very taken*) Odso, Liversausage! What a corking bit of scrummage!

Song 10 (Donna Estella)

Donna Estella Pliz. Do as Don Iguana says, leave thees place. Per favor.

Polperro I don't think I have had the pleasure. Your name, madam?

Donna Estella I am Donna Estella Del Torremolinos y Chimichanga, niece to Hees Exellencee the Viceroy of the Spaneesh Eendies. My guardian, Don Iguana, and I were passengers aboard the treasure galleon *Santa Maria* bound for Spain, when a great storm wrecked our vessel, and we were cast upon thees croo-el an' eenhospeetable shore.

Polperro Madam, I'm yours, and so forth. What the devil's the matter with your countryman? Does he have the vapours?

Donna Estella I am afraid that he swallowed too much sea water when we were shippa-wreck-ed.

Liversausage My dear lady, we are *not* privateers — but I fear that a party of quite vile buccaneers may indeed be on their way here, even as we speak. I would urge you to admit us, so that we may look to the defence of the stockade.

Donna Estella We weel take-a our chances with these men. Now pliz, mi Capitan, leave us.

Polperro But if we could just get our ship back, we could bring you off this wretched island. Safe passage and all that. Word of honour.

Don Iguana (*crowing*) He's feeb-bing!

Polperro (*losing his temper*) Now look 'ee, you deranged, onion-eating twerp, say but one word more, and I'll make you wish you'd never left the family tapas bar in Old Seville!

Donna Estella H-why should I beleeve you?

Polperro Would I be here wasting my time talking to a washed-up Spanish omelette like him, unless it was true?

Don Iguana Ah, shove off Eengleesh heretic! I hope you choke on your afternoon tea and muffin!

Polperro But you're in danger!

Donna Estella We are grateful for your concern, señor, but we must remain. Adios.

Liversausage Come, Polperro. They won't be helped. We must leave them. Let us find the others.

Don Iguana (*triumphantly*) Via con Dios, Roas' bif! See you in hell!

Polperro Rot me! What an extraordinary chap!

Don Iguana Hey, hombré! Next time you are in Caracas, don't forget to look me up at the Pina Colada Club! Olé!

Smellit That's the Spanish for you sir — unpredictable blighters.

Polperro Yes. Jolly good job we sank their Armadillo.

Smellit Armada.

Polperro (*interested*) We sank that as well, did we?

They go off

The Lights fade to Black-out

SCENE 3

Another part of the island

As the Lights come up, the tropical paradise sound effects first encountered near the end of Act I are still in full spate

Nancy and the Dame enter, peering around at the strange equatorial foliage

Dame Well, this *is* a peculiar place, and no mistake. I keep expectin' to bump into David Attenborough.

Nancy At least we seem to have shaken off our pursuers.

Dame Yes. Let's see if we can find Jim and the others.

Nancy I don't know *what* Papa is going to say when he sees me.

Dame That's the least of our worries.

There is a sudden, furtive movement, close at hand

Hang on. What was that?
Nancy What was what?
Dame That! (*Bellowing in sudden panic*) Aaaarrrgggh!

. *The wild figure of Bertha Gunn leaps out in front of them. She has a tangled mass of white hair topping off a bizarre patchwork outfit apparently composed of bits of sailcloth and goatskin, ship's cordage and coconut husks, all held together by rabbit droppings. She windmills long, skinny arms, whilst hopping from foot to foot, jabbering manically*

Bertha Gunn (*shrieking*) Trolley!
Dame Oh Gawd! You gave me such a fright, jumping out like that! Who are you?
Bertha Gunn Who am I! Who am I? sez you, wi' a hey-rig-a-jig ... I'm Bertha I am, sez I ... Poor Bertha Gunn ... And it's pleased I am to know 'ee, sez you — belike ...
Dame (*to the audience*) Ruddy heck! I got more sense out of the perishin' parrot!
Nancy What on earth are you doing on this island? Were you shipwrecked?
Bertha Gunn Nay, matey. Marooned. Three years since, and never a bite o' a Christian diet in all that time ... (*Whining*) You mightn't happen to have a lump o' bread puddin' about you now? Many's the long night I dreamed on bread puddin' ... Oh, I allus had a tray o' cold bread puddin' on my tea trolley.
Dame Cold bread puddin'! Yuck! Great slabs of grey, greasy stodge.
Bertha Gunn (*salivating*) Wi' cold lumpy custard ... Or onion gravy ...
Dame She's potty. I'm off.
Nancy Hold on. (*To Bertha*) Now look 'ee, old loon, shouldn't castaways hanker after a piece of honest Cheddar — or roast beef of Olde England?
Bertha Gunn Cheese, sez you! Oh ay! Some folks might dream on cheese, I 'spect, or roast 'tatties — or even choc'late. Now Squint, he were yer main man fer choc'late, so 'e was.
Dame You knew Squint!
Bertha Gunn Knew him, sez you? I wuz 'is tea lady, by thunder! Aboard his old ship: *The Yorkie*. Always handy me, wi' a nice mug o' splosh, and a packet o' choccy digestives on me trolley, fer the long watches o' the night. Oh ay, I knowed Squint well enough, and all 'is willainous crew. 'Ere! You bain't wi' Squint's crew, be ye, shipmates?
Nancy No. But I fancy that there are some of Squint's old hands ashore.
Bertha Gunn (*trembling spastically*) Not a man — wi' one leg?
Dame Slither?

Bertha Gunn That's him! Oh! He's an awful bad sort, ladies! A terrible hard
man. And allus wi' a plank about him.
Dame (*bitterly*) Tell me about it! I've still got seaweed in me stays. But how
on earth did you get here?
Bertha Gunn Like I sez, I were Squint's tea lady on his last voyage. Billy
Fishbones were the mate, Long John, 'e wuz quartermaster, and Israel Feet
the bosun. I wuz aboard when Squint put in here to stow his treasure chest
— after the plunderin' o' Panama. Him and six big strappin' lads went
ashore wi' the loot, and come sundown, back marches Squint, and all
alone. T' other six he skewered and filleted, I shouldn't wonder. So, we puts
out fer Tortuga, wi' not another word said — an' that wuz that. Then, three
year back, I were tea lady on this other ship, d'ye see, an' we sighted this
selfsame island. "'Ere!" sez I. "That there's the very place where old Squint
parked his booty. Let's put ashore and find it." (*Mournfully*) But we
couldn't find it, and after seven days o' diggin', they up an left in a right
old lather. "You want the blessed booty, Bertha Gunn," sez they, "then you
stay 'ere and dig fer it!" An' away they sailed, and I bin here ever since —
an' never a sniff o' bread puddin' the while. (*Beginning to snivel*) And now,
Long John Slither's abroad, and we'll all end up as shark's food, an' poor
Bertha Gunn won't never get to taste a lump o' that stodgy ol' bread
puddin' ever again ...
Nancy Now don't take on so. We'll trounce Slither and his band of plaguey
rascals yet. For my father, the squire, is also ashore — and he's justice of
the peace, d'ye see, so he'll jolly well sort these fellows out, and sharpish
I shouldn't wonder. And when we all get home to Old England, and they're
dangling in chains from execution dock, you Bertha, shall have bread
pudding of the very best — and off a silver dish, I warrant.
Bertha Gunn Really?
Nancy On my oath, madam!
Dame That's the ticket. Here, I know, how about a bit of a sing-song to keep
our spirits up, eh?
Bertha Gunn Oooh yes! Singin'! I bain't heard a Christian voice raised in
melodious harmony these three years since.
Dame Yes. Well ... I wouldn't hold my breath if I were you. Look! We can
get the mob to join in! What do you say, folks? How's about a little sing
along, eh? Just to cheer our new chum up? That's the spirit! Who'd like to
come on up then?

And so on

Song 11 (Audience participation song)

*Followed by handout of sweets, rounds of applause from adoring parents,
etc., etc.*

Bertha Gunn Oh! Don't I feel mighty cheered up now, sez you? I should
think I do, sez I, and wi' a vengeance, by the powers. (*To Nancy*) Now hark
'ee, miss, when you finds your father, the squire, you say to him: "Bertha
Gunn ain't been idle these three years." You tell 'im that, miss. "Bertha
Gunn ain't been idle."

Dame Well aren't you coming with us? You can tell him yourself. We're
heading for the old stockade.

Bertha Gunn Me? No, no — not I! I got 'mportant business to attend to, I
has! I'll see you later shipmates

Bertha Gunn scuttles off

Dame Ah well. Daft as a brush. Still, never mind — let's try and find Jim
and yer pa.

Sudden crash of musketry from nearby

Nancy Merciful heavens! Something's afoot!

Dame Yes ... About twelve inches to be precise. Come on, let's get out of
here!

They exit

The Lights fade to Black-out

SCENE 4

And another part of the island

*Denoted by different lighting and sound effects — i.e. turn up the volume on
cicadas, turn down the volume on waves lapping on the seashore*

Jim, Bodmin and Newquay enter, all looking distinctly uneasy

Bodmin I don't like it. I definitely do not like it. That was musketry, and it
wasn't very far away neither.

Newquay I want to go home.

Jim Bravely now, lads. Be of stout heart.

Bodmin Oh don't you start! You're beginning to sound like that pesky sea
captain: "cheerily" this, and "yarely" that. I mean, it's all very well for him,
but I never entered domestic service for this, you know. I just wanted to be
— a gentleman's gentleman.

Newquay All I ever wanted to be, was a flunkey. I was quite happy flunkin'.
Now I'm in a bloomin' war zone. And I'm starvin' — I could even eat one
of your mum's rotten fisherman's pies.

Jim I am a trifle peckish, I must admit. I know! Mother prepared a packed
lunch for me before we left the ship. Here we are. (*He rummages in his
knapsack*) Gosh! Look! The map! I had it all the time! Mother must have
hidden it in there for safekeeping.

Bodmin Safekeeping? Oh, yes, well, of course, it's safe as the Bank of
England here with us, isn't it? I mean, in the middle of a hostile jungle,
pursued by an entire convention of ruthless cutthroats, and defended by
one pimply youth ——

Newquay That's you.

Bodmin And two frightened flunkeys ——

Newquay That's us.

Jim Courage, lads! Listen!

Piratical voices can be heard "ha-harring" just off stage

They're coming! Now, men, I intend to effect an ambuscade.

Bodmin (*drily*) That's nice. An ambuscade.

Jim Here they come!

Bodmin Here they come. Ready, Mr Newquay?

Newquay Ready, Mr Bodmin.

Bodmin Right then.

Newquay } (*together*) Run for it!
Bodmin

Newquay and Bodmin flee in a frightful funk

Jim is left standing alone, pistol raised in one hand, map clutched in the other

*The Pirates, led by Long John Slither, emerge into the clearing, Donna
Estella Del Torremolinos y Chimichanga dishevelled amongst them, a
rope tied about her waist, the other end held by Pink Dog*

Jim Mr Slither! Stand and deliver, sir! Or I let fly with fire and shot!

Slither (*apparently delighted*) Jim! Jim Ladd! Aaar, well I'm right glad to
see you cully. I was mortal afeared you'd got yourself lost, d'ye see.

Jim It's no use, Mr Slither, I know your true colours — and they are black
as hell's mouth.

Slither (*reasonably*) Now, Jim, I allus liked you — right from the first.
"There's a boy," sez I, "as reminds me o' meself when I were a nipper."
You an' me, Jim, we could be firm friends, by thunder. It's not too late for
you to jine, Jim — to take your share, an' die a gennelman.

Jim I don't think so, sir.

Slither D'ye not? (*Peering closely*) Ah, well ... And what might that be, as is a clutched in your sticky little hand?

Israel (*goggling*) By all the powers, John, 'tis the map! The cub's got the blessed treasure map!

Slither (*eyes gleaming*) Is that a fact?

He makes to step forward. Jim aims his pistol

Jim Take but one step more, sir, and I'll put a pistol ball square between your shifty eyes.

Slither (*after a pause*) Well now — you're a young, tight fellow, to be sure. Ah, me. 'Tis pity you ain't dishonest, Jim, for I'd as soon have you on my side. But, there it is.

Jim Who's the lady?

Slither Just a little Spanish señorita, as we found a-hidin' in the old stockade. We'm taken her under tow, on the offchance that she might be worth a few pesos prize money.

Donna Estella (*spitting rage*) You feelthy peeg! Caramba! You weel leeve to regret thees! I weel keel you!

Slither (*wiping his eye*) Sparky, ain't she? She had some other loopy donkey wi' her — but we had to knock him down wi' a marlinspike. Kept on lobbin' blessed coconuts at us! Left him fer dead, so we did!

Jim You villain. Release the lady!

Slither Why should I? (*Slyly*) Tell 'ee what though, I'll trade her — fer the map.

Jim Never! You'll release her anyway — or rue the day!

Slither Well now. You taken a shine to her have 'ee, Jim Ladd? An' here's me thinkin' you wuz sweet on young Dick, the ship's boy. Or should I say — the lovely Nancy.

The Pirates all hoot with mocking laughter

Jim (*aghast*) Nancy! Then you know! What have you done with her, you fiend?

Slither (*lying fluently*) Oh, I got her stowed away safe, and that's how she'll stay. Providin' you hands over that there map!

Jim Never!

Slither Reckon the poor girl must be a mite cramped down in they scuppers, in the dark — wi' only the rats fer company.

Jim You'll free her? Word of honour?

Slither Cross me heart, and hopes to die.

Jim And you'll release this lady, into the bargain?

Slither My word on't.
Jim Very well. Here. Take the map.

Jim holds the map out and lowers his pistol. Slither takes the proffered map

Slither Why, thank you sir, and kindly. (*And sticks his pistol into Jim's ear.
Snarling*) Now drop your pistol, you young villain!
Jim (*shocked*) But you gave your word!
Slither Oh ay. But then, I am a lyin', thievin', deceitful, murderous dog, ain't
I? Ha ha ha!

*Audience participation, as the Pirates all roar with laughter. Israel plucks
Jim's pistol away*

Groundbait, rope 'em up together, whiles I take a gander at the chart! (*He
unfolds the map to peruse it*)

Groundbait hustles Jim over to be roped to Donna Estella

Let's see ... Ah, yes. Tall tree, Spyglass hill. One hundred paces, Nor', by
Nor'-East.
Israel Feet (*peering over Slither's shoulder*) Nor', by Nor'-East? Be you
sure, John? You'm a blessed sea-cook ar'ter all, not a navigator. I'll just
take a squint, shall I?
Slither (*jerking the map from Israel's reach*) Lay aft, you maggot! I can read
a poxy chart, can't I? Leastways, I should think I could! (*Surreptitiously
turning the map around several times in an attempt to understand it*) Nor',
by Nor'-East! Right, lads, march on. We wasted enough time already! Ha
ha ha!

They exit to audience participation

The Lights fade to Black-out

SCENE 5

Another part of the island nearby

The Lights come up

Polperro, Liversausage and Smellit enter

Polperro Well, I fancy the fireworks were coming from the stockade. Our Spanish friends have succumbed, I daresay.

Bodmin and Newquay burst on from the other direction, still running

Redruth!

Bodmin attempts to speak, but can only gasp raggedly for breath

Newquay (*puffing, but managing to object on Bodmin's behalf*) Bodmin, sir.
Polperro Where's young Jim?
Bodmin (*gradually recovering*) Jim? Oh — Jim! He's er — back there, sir, with the, er — what d'you call 'em. Who are those men he's with, Mr Newquay? The, um ... The, er ...
Newquay Pirates.
Bodmin Pirates! That's it! He's with the, er — pirates.
Polperro (*outraged*) You abandoned him!
Newquay Oh no, sir! We didn't abandon him. It's just that we ran away rather fast.
Bodmin And he didn't.
Polperro Redruth, you craven poltroon!
Bodmin (*correcting him*) Bodmin, you craven poltroon, sir.
Polperro Gadzooks sirrah! How could you be so lily-livered! Where's your spunk, man?

Bodmin and Newquay hastily consult in whispers. Bodmin looks up and clears his throat

Bodmin Newquay and I can only offer one conceivable explanation, Squire.
Polperro Well?
Bodmin We're a pair of snivelling cowards, sir.
Polperro Plainly.
Liversausage Oh don't be too hard on the fellows, Polperro. After all, one's your blessed Under-Butler, and the other's your Head Gardener. You can hardly expect your household flunkeys to acquit themselves with honour on the field of battle!
Polperro Pah! Abject deserters! I've a mind to maroon the scoundrels here as punishment.
Newquay (*flinging himself down at Polperro's feet*) Oh no! Please, sir. Not that! Don't maroon me. I couldn't stand it — it's not my colour.
Polperro Be silent!
Bodmin Beggin' the admiral's pardon, but there is just one other small circumstance we ought to mention.

Polperro This had better be good.

Bodmin Young Jim's got the treasure map.

Polperro *What!* But I thought the dragon had it!

Bodmin Apparently not, sir. She er — used it to wrap the lad's sandwiches, sir.

Polperro (*apoplectic*) His sandwiches! You utter blaggards! Are you telling me, you not only abandoned the boy, but Squint's map to boot?

Bodmin Er — yes sir. I think that about sums it up, sir.

Liversausage Well, what now? Do we rescue Jim, or make another attempt at the stockade?

Polperro Oh, absolutely no question, Liversausage! We must save the boy.

Liversausage Ah yes, of course. *Noblesse oblige* and all that. You feel responsible, I suppose.

Polperro Stuff responsible — he's got the ruddy treasure map! Come on!

They all exit hurriedly

The Lights fade to Black-out

SCENE 6

Another part of the island

The Lights come up on Jim and Donna Estella sitting in gloomy silence. They have been left momentarily unguarded, but are still joined by a length of rope

Bertha Gunn is hidden from view behind some nearby bushes

Donna Estella Pliz. I would like to thank you for tryeeng to help me. Now you are een beeg trouble also. And Los Bandidos have your treasure map, no?

Jim Yes. Still, I was in beeg trouble already. I'm just sorry you've been dragged into it.

Donna Estella Oh Jeem! I have been so stupeed! We should have fled the stockado weeth your friend, the English Milord. Then Don Iguana would not have hees head bashed een, I would not be een the veelainous clutches of the hayt-ful desperadoes, and they would not have your map.

Jim Chin up, Estella! All still to play for. I do not doubt but that Squire Polperro and his companions will come to our aid, and as for your friend — well, I wager he wakes up with a headache, nothing more.

Donna Estella Ah, Jeem. You are so kind. So gallant. A true caballero.

Jim A what?

Donna Estella How you say? A k-nigget in shineeng armour.

Jim Oh, I see.

Donna Estella Tell me. Who ees thees Nancee I hear you speak of?

Jim Oh, um ... No-one really. Just a friend. She's the squire's daughter actually.

Donna Estella And she ees your lay-dee, yes?

Jim No. Well, not exactly. She's rather struck on me, but then I'm just an impoverished pleb — while she's a noble lady of title and fortune. I don't really think there's much future in it.

Donna Estella Nobeelity, Jeem, ees not een a man's blood, but een hees heart, and een hees deeds. You are worthy *h*of any lay-dee.

Jim Well, it's terribly nice of you to say so, but I'm not at all sure I want all her money and estates. You see, I rather like being ordinary.

Donna Estella You are far from that, I theenk.

Jim Really?

Donna Estella You betta beleeve it, amigo.

Jim Gosh.

And so, we finally arrive at the inevitable slushy duet, although not for Jim and Nancy, as may have been anticipated, but somewhat unexpectedly, for Jim and his new chum, the ravishing Spanish beauty — who has obviously taken something of a shine to our lad

Song 12 (Jim and Donna Estella)

Slither and the Pirates enter when the song has finished

Slither (*abruptly*) Bah! Stow that racket! Pathetic lovelorn mewling! Right, shipmates. Long John's got this here map all figured out now — and I fancy that Squint's gold is buried right here, beneath our very feet. Hard by Skull Rock.

Israel Feet (*still trying to peer at the map*) Sure?

Slither Course I'm sure, you lugworm!

Israel Feet Why then — let's dig her up, by thunder!

Pink Dog Right you are Israel! Lay to all hands!

Music, as the Pirates do a bit of token scrabbling around in the sand to reveal a large pit, into which they eagerly peer

George Merry It's gone! There ain't nothin' down there, John! Just a girt big 'ole!

Israel Feet We been daddled, John! Someone's got here afore us!

Slither (*crumpling up the chart and tossing it aside*) So much for that!

Groundbait That boy — drat him! From first to last we've come to grief upon him!

Pink Dog We have that, by thunder! He's hazed us long enough! I say we spills his giblets, and wi' no more ado!

George Merry I seconds that!

Pirates (*collectively*) Aaar.

Slither What? Squander an 'ostage! Be you daft, or what?

Groundbait Belay that, John! We means to have his heart out, and there's an end to it!

Slither Oho! Maybe you thought you was cap'n here, Seamus O' Flaherty? You're a pushin' lad to be sure.

Israel Feet All right, mates — no need for cross words. We needs cool heads for this business. This place gives me the blessed willies, John. Let's get out of here, eh?

George Merry Ay. If this is where Squint planted his treasure, then this is where them six poor lads met their grisly end, you may lay to that.

Slither Aaar, stow yer bleatin'! Squint's gone, shipmates — he won't come hazin' us no more.

A horrible, rasping voice suddenly echoes eerily around the grove

Voice "Fifteen men on a dead man's chest! Yo ho ho, and a bottle of rum ..."

Israel Feet (*thunderstruck*) It's Squint! "Fifteen Men" was allus his fav'rite song!

Slither Squint's dead, I tell 'ee, and gone to hell. It's a trick o' the imagination. Nothin' more.

Voice "Drink and the devil had done for the rest! Yo ho ho, and a bottle of rum!"

George Merry 'Tis a ghost right enough, mates. Squint's ghost!

Slither Belay that talk! Superstitious claptrap! There ain't no such thing as ghosts!

Voice "Blood and blue water! Blood and blue water!" Ha ha ha ha ha!

Israel Feet "Blood and blue water!" Them was 'is last words above board! 'Tis Squint's spirit, sure as night follows day!

Slither Well I don't hold with no spirits — Squint or no Squint. I never was afeared o' him in life, and by the powers, I'll face him dead!

Israel Feet Stow that, John! Don't you go tangling with no ghosts. 'Tis powerful bad luck for a seafarin' man.

Slither Ghosts be damned! That there's a 'uman voice, and you may lay to that! Someone's a joshin' us, by thunder!

*He dives into the nearby bushes, and after a very brief scuffle, drags out
Bertha Gunn, clutching her by the scrag of her scrawny neck*

Well look 'ee here! Sink me, if it ain't Bertha Gunn!
Bertha Gunn (*gibbering with fear*) Art'noon, Mr Slither, sez I, an' art'noon,
Bertha, sez you! Long time no see, sez I, and happen you couldn't give a
monkeys, sez you.

*Slither stuffs the muzzle of his flintlock pistol into her mouth, abruptly
silencing her blithering. Bertha regards him, bug-eyed, along the barrel of
his pistol*

Slither Shut it! Well, lads, there's your blessed ghost! Squint's old tea lady
no less! Satisfied? I can't hear no more ghostly voices, can you? (*After a
pause*) There now, I think we can ——
Voice "Blood and blue water!" Ha ha ha ha!
Pink Dog (*shaken*) The devil, John! That's Squint's voice!
George Merry That's Squint right enough. 'Tain't another man livin', as
could carry him off so well.
Israel Feet His ghost walks! Rot you, John Slither! Ye've challenged the
spirit world, and now we'm all doomed!
Groundbait Israel's right, lads! 'Tis the curse o' Squint's gold! We'd best
flee!
Slither Stand firm, ye dogs! By heaven, I'll put a bullet in the first man as
runs!
Israel Feet Better a bullet, than dance a hornpipe wi' the devil hisself, eh
shipmates?
George Merry You're right there, Israel!
Groundbait Abandon ship, lads!
Pink Dog Run for it!

The Pirates flee off L

Slither You spineless jellyfish! I'll have you keelhauled for this! 'Tis
mutiny, by thunder! Wait 'til I gets you back in Port Royal! I'll give you
ghosts right enough — you gutless rabble!
Polperro (*off*) Jim! Jim Ladd!
Slither (*looking toward the voices*) Well, well! Rescued in the nick, I reckon,
young Jim. So 'tis farewell and adieu for the moment, shipmate, but you
ain't seen the last o' John Slither — and you may lay to that! Ha ha ha!

Audience participation

Slither stumps quickly off L

A moment later, Squire Polperro and his party enter R

Liversausage Jim! Thank heavens you're safe.
Polperro And, señorita! Delighted to find you in good health, ma'am, I was
afraid that ... Rat me! There goes Slither! Look lively, Smellit — you might
still wing the blighter!

Smellit takes aim with his musket

Jim No, Captain! Don't shoot! I must tell you, gentlemen, that Long John
Slither saved our lives earlier — why, I cannot fathom, but save us he
certainly did.
Smellit But why did the villains take flight so suddenly? I fancied we had
a battle-royal upon our hands.
Jim A remarkable thing, sir. They supposed they heard the ghost of Captain
Squint.
Polperro Ghosts! Pshaw! Stuff 'n' nonsense! Frightened of their own
shadows most like. Typical, weasely Frenchies.
Jim No, sir. I cannot account for it, but there *was* a voice. Quite terrible. I
heard it with my own ears.
Smellit Well, whatever the cause of their fright, you may be sure the villains
will regroup, sir — at the stockade, I shouldn't wonder.
Polperro Most like. (*Catching sight of Bertha Gunn*) And who is this?
Bertha Gunn Who is this? sez you, wi' a rollickin' randy-dandy-o! 'Tis poor
Bertha Gunn, sez I, as ain't had a bite o' cold bread puddin' for three long
year. An' you must be the Squire Polperro, sez I, and it's pleased I am to
meet 'ee, sez you — an' you wouldn't happen to have a slice o' cold bread
puddin' secreted about your worshipful person — now would you?
Polperro (*amazed*) Stone me!
Liversausage I take it this is where the treasure was hid, Jim. I suppose the
rascals have made off with it?
Jim Oh no, sir. The treasure was already gone!
Polperro Gone! How?
Bertha Gunn Aha! That a'minds me. Poor Bertha Gunn's got a 'mportant
mess'ge, so she has.
Polperro A message? For whom?
Bertha Gunn For whom? sez you. Why for you, sez I. In a manner o'
speakin'.
Polperro (*trying very hard to be patient*) Well — and who is this message
from?
Bertha Gunn Who's it from? sez you. An' you may well ask, sez I. Who
is it from? Oh, er ... (*She scratches her head, and eventually remembers*)
Me!
Polperro And?

Bertha Gunn And what?

Polperro (*shouting*) What's the ruddy message, you loopy old scarecrow!

Bertha Gunn Oh, that. It was: "Bertha Gunn ain't been idle these three years." Leastways, I think that was the message.

Polperro Well it was *your* message — don't you know! Oh never mind! What does it mean?

Bertha Gunn Wossit mean? (*Smugly*) Means I done moved the blessed treasure, don't it.

Polperro *You* moved it! Where to?

Bertha Gunn The stockade.

All The stockade!

They all charge off, desparate to reach the stockade before the mutineers

After a moment or two, there is a minor commotion in the undergrowth, and a giant crimson form emerges, flapping its wings, Cap'n Haddock peers about with mild interest

Cap'n Haddock Aaark! "Blood and Blue Water! Blood and Blue Water!" Aaark! Ha ha ha ha!

His beady eye alights upon the discarded treasure map. He stoops to retrieve it before wandering off

The Lights fade to Black-out

SCENE 7

The Denouement

The Lights come up on the stockade. There is no sign of life, the gate still firmly closed

Polperro and his party enter

Polperro (*calling*) Hallo! I say! Anyone at home?

The Dame appears behind the palisade

Dame Oh, hallo Squire. Took your blinkin' time, didn't you?

Jim Mum!

Dame Hallo, Jimbo! How's your luck?

Liversausage Thank heavens you're safe, ma'am!

Dame Oh, you don't want to worry about me, Doc. I can look after meself.

Smellit But what happened to the pirates?

Dame Dunno. When we got here, the place was deserted — except for this Spanish geezer with a bump the size of an ostrich egg on his bonce! Here he is. Feelin' any better?

Don Iguana appears beside the Dame, head bandaged, and a rueful smile on his face

Don Iguana Buenos dias, señors.

Donna Estella Don Iguana! You are alive!

Don Iguana By the grace of God — and thanks to these lovelee lay-dees.

Polperro Ladies? What ladies?

Dame (*quickly*) He means me.

Polperro You're no lady! Besides, he said lad*ies*.

Dame Ah yes. I've got someone I'd like you to meet.

Nancy appears sheepishly from behind the palisade

Nancy Hiya, Pops.

Jim (*relieved*) Nancy!

Polperro Nancy! S'death, child! What are you doing here!

Nancy I stowed away.

Polperro But I expressly forbade you to come!

Nancy (*flaring*) Exactly.

Polperro Garzoon! I don't know, Liversausage! Young people today! It wasn't like this when I was a boy. The Seventeen-Sixties have got a lot to answer for ——

Smellit (*interrupting*) Tell me, ma'am, did not the pirates return?

Dame Pirates? Oh them, yes. They been comin' all afternoon — but I saw 'em off.

Liversausage Saw 'em off? But you were armed only with coconuts!

Dame Ah yes, but what they didn't know, was that when I was a girl in (*local town*) I was coconut-shy champion at the (*local fair*) for seven years on the trot! (*She catches sight of Bertha Gunn*) Hallo Bertha! You give His Nibs your message then?

Polperro Don't tell me you're acquainted with this infernal nanny goat!

Dame Who, Bertha? Oh yes.

Polperro Fine. Well perhaps you can get her to explain where she buried the treasure!

Dame Oooh! It's here is it? I should have known you'd found it, you old minx! Where'd you put it, Bertha?

Bertha Gunn Put it over there, didn't I. Below deck. (*She points to an area of plank flooring alongside the stockade*)
Polperro Under the duckboards?
Bertha Gunn That's it! Quack! Quack!
Polperro Right, lads! Get to it!

Bodmin and Newquay swiftly lift a section of decking to reveal a pit. The Dame hurriedly makes her way down from the palisade, and pushes to the front to stand beside Polperro, who is peering into the cavity

Dame Let me through. I've come a long way for this.
Polperro (*doubtfully*) Are you quite sure this is where you buried the treasure?
Bertha Gunn Oh yes.
Polperro But there's nothing there. Just thousands of little pieces of — what looks like tin foil.
Bertha Gunn S'right.
Dame And a great slimy pool of festerin' sludge.
Polperro Well, where's the blessed loot? Where's Squint's treasure?
Bertha Gunn Well, that's it. It's there, ain't it.
Polperro I don't get it.
Liversausage (*starting to laugh*) Ha ha! Oh ha ha ha! Squint's treasure! Ha ha ha ha!
Polperro (*annoyed*) Rot me, Liversausage! This is no time for you to suddenly develop a sense of humour! There's supposed to be a fortune in gold and silver coin down there!
Liversausage Oh, it's coin all right. Chocolate coin! Don't you see, Polperro? Squint's treasure was chocolate money!
Polperro Chocolate!
Dame Chocolate!
Donna Estella Chocolado!
Jim Chocolate! Of course! What was it Billy Fishbones said? Squint had a wicked passion for chocolate!
Nancy Yes! And Bertha! What did you tell us? Squint was a main man for chocolate!
Polperro Chocolate! You mean I've come all this blessed way, and at monstrous expense, just to find Squint's hidden treasure trove of maggoty chocolate!
Liversausage I'm afraid it rather looks like it.
Polperro I think I'm going to be sick.
Bodmin So all that gloop at the bottom of the pit must be ...
Dame That's right. Melted choccy. Must be twenty gallons of the stuff.
Bertha Gunn Melted, sez you! Oh ay. 'Twas the heat o' the sun, sez I. Started meltin' soon as I dug 'er up, didn't she — made a pretty mess o' my goatskins, I can tell 'ee.

Liversausage What now, Polperro? (*Gesturing to the hole*) There's nothing for us here.

Polperro 'Tis plain.

Dame No. I think you'll find 'tis milk actually. (*Boom Boom!*) Milk — plain — chocolate. Geddit? Oh never mind. We're nearly finished anyway.

Abruptly, the Pirates appear, led by Long John Slither, his pistol pointed at Polperro

Sllither And you may lay to that, shipmates! Now put 'em up! We'll take charge o' the booty.

Dame Well, well. If it isn't the one-legged bandit.

Smellit Slither, for your own sake, I advise you to come no closer. Your crew may not like what they find.

Israel Feet What's he mean, John?

Slither Bah! He hazin' us, by thunder.

Smellit Very well, but don't say I didn't warn you. You want Squint's treasure? Then take it. You're welcome to it!

Slither (*taken aback*) Eh?

Israel Feet Somethin's amiss, John.

Pink Dog Take a gander, shipmates.

The mutineers peer suspiciously into the hole

Smellit Well, my lads. You sailed with Squint. I hope you know what became of all the gold the old devil plundered — for all that's buried here is his tuck box.

Israel Feet 'Tis chocolate! 'Tis blessed choccy, by the powers!

Slither (*thunderstruck*) Chocolate!

Groundbait And never a silver halfpenny to be seen!

Israel Feet This is your fortune is it, John Slither! This is the rich booty, as us poor lads laid our precious necks on the line for!

Pink Dog An' fer what! I'll tell you fer what! Fer half a ton o' liquidized Bourneville, that's what!

Slither Well, how wuz I to know?

Israel Feet You brought us here! You dragged us halfway round the poxy globe fer nothin' — you wooden-headed lubber!

Groundbait (*gravely*) Shipmates, there be only one course left to us.

Pink Dog You're right there, Groundbait.

Israel Feet Give it him now — and no goin' back.

Slither Now, lads. Let's not be hasty.

Groundbait Ship's Council 'as spoken, John Slither. Show us yer paw. (*He holds out a small square of paper*) Here be your ticket.

Slither (*trembling*) Bound for where, shipmates?

Groundbait thrusts the scrap of paper into Long John's hand

Groundbait The passage to hell.
Slither (*horrified*) No! No! Not the Pink Spot, mates! Not to your old cap'n.
Israel Feet Belay that, John Slither! This here crew has tipped you the Pink
Spot, and you be cap'n no longer!
Slither No! Not the Pink Spot! Noooooo!

*With a cry of horror, he backs away, loses his footing, and tumbles
backwards into the pit, falling from view with a strangled yell*

Jim (*starting forward*) Mr Slither!
Liversausage No, Jim. Let the rogues settle their own account. They'll all
answer to the proper authorities soon enough.
Jim What do you mean?

The opening strains of "Rule Britannia" are distantly heard

Nancy Listen!
Polperro Hark 'ee! What's that?

"Rule Britannia" grows louder

Smellit Unless I'm very much mistaken, sir, I think you will find "that" is
His Majesty's Royal Navy — The Jamaica Squadron, to be precise —
standing out for Kingston town. A dozen stout ships o' the line, riding
proud upon the mighty billow, mainsails full, gunports open, and decks
cleared down for action, white ensigns a-streaming in the wind. Just in the
nick of time, as usual.

George Merry runs on

George Merry We'm scuppered, shipmates! 'Tis the Navy!
Pink Dog A frigate?
George Merry Stow frigate! 'Tis a whole blessed squadron, by thunder!
Abandon ship, me hearties! Head for the hills!

*"Rule Britannia" concludes. The band break into a brisk rendition of
"Hearts of Oak" during the following*

Groundbait What about Long John?

Pink Dog Leave him!
Israel Feet He can stew in his own chocolate sauce!
George Merry Come on! Run!

The Pirates turn and flee

Polperro I say! The Navy! Jolly good!
Liversausage Wait a moment! What about Slither?

They gather around the hole

Bodmin He's gone.
Newquay Sunk without trace.
Jim Hold on! What's that?!

Jim reaches down and pulls up a crutch covered in melted chocolate. All regard the bizarre object in silence for a moment

Dame Oooh! What a way to go! Death by chocolate. I always knew he'd come to a sticky end. (*To the audience*) Sticky end! Geddit? These are the jokes, folks! Oh, forget it.
Liversausage Well, Polperro, what next? The lost city of Eldorado?
Polperro I don't think so, Liversausage. I've had enough adventures for a while. Old England beckons — a pint of Old Wallop, and me armchair by the fire.
Nancy I shan't be coming home with you, Papa. Don Iguana wishes to show me the extent of his haciendas.
Dame (*aside*) I bet he does.
Nancy (*slipping her arm through Don Iguana's*) And naturally, I have accepted his offer of lavish hospitality. Don Iguana and I have much in common.
Polperro Yes — you both give me the pip! If you seriously think I'm letting you take up with some crackpot Spaniard, my girl — you're as barmy as he is!
Nancy He's not a crackpot! (*Stamping her foot*) Honestly Daddy! He's perfectly charming.
Don Iguana (*smoothly*) If I insulted you earlier, señor, I must apologize. I can assure you, the crack on the head I received from these villains, has fully restored my senses.
Polperro (*fuming*) Egad! If there's one thing I hate more than a barking mad Spaniard, it's a nauseatingly civil Spaniard!
Nancy Did you know, Papa, that Don Iguana is the wealthiest man in all Spain?

Polperro On the other hand, one has to set aside old quarrels.

Nancy He has a fortune in excess of seventeen million pesos.

Dame (*to the audience*) That's about twenty-six p.

Polperro But wait a moment! What about young Jim? I thought you were sweet on him.

Nancy I am! I mean ... well — he is sweet ... just rather, um — poor.

Jim It's all right, Squire. I don't mind, really I don't. I'm just glad that Nancy has found someone equally, ah — uncommon.

Donna Estella Don Iguana, I *h*am so happee for you. I, too, have found romance on thees meesteerious island — in the person of a gallant Eengleesh gentleman.

Polperro (*puffing up*) I say!

Donna Estella Handsome ...

Polperro Rather!

Donna Estella Courageous ...

Polperro Natch.

Donna Estella And young.

Polperro (*double take*) Eh?

Donna Estella I have found true love. And that ees worth more than any crock of gold. Jeem, weel you be my own caballero?

Polperro (*spluttering*) Jim? Jim? But he's — he's ...

Donna Estella Si, señor?

Polperro He's a, er — (*giving in gracefully*) a fine, upstanding young fellow — sharp as a knife.

Jim (*bowing*) My lady.

Dame Oh no you don't, my lad! I'm not havin' you bringin' some exotic, foreign dolly home to *The Admirable Bimbo* — stinkin' out my nice clean scullery with sardines and garlic!

Don Iguana Señora, I should tell you that which Donna Estella has neeglected to mention — that she ees een fac', the wealthiest wooman een all España.

Dame Is that a fact? You know, I could get used to sardines.

Liversausage What about the mutineers?

Smellit Leave the Navy to sort 'em out. We can sail the ship home without 'em — if all hands are willing to pull together?

Dame Ooh yes! (*Suggestively*) I'm willing to pull — Skipper.

Smellit Explain yourself, madam.

Dame Oh, come on, Smelly — you po-faced old sea dog you! Don't tell me you don't find me just the teensy-weensiest bit attractive?

Smellit (*stiffly*) Madam, I'd rather court a Portuguese Man o' War.

Dame (*confused*) A foreign galleon?

Smellit A large, poisonous jellyfish.

Dame (*ever hopeful*) I suppose a snog's out of the question then.

Bertha Gunn 'Ere! 'ow 'bout poor Bertha Gunn, shipmates? What's to become o' her?

Dame Well, there's a nice old pub in Bristol Docks needs a new landlady. The old landlord got himself barred. (*To the audience*) Barred! Chocolate! Geddit? Chocolate bar — see? Oh, I don't know why I bother with you lot.

Bodmin Well, Mr Newquay, looks like we're on our way home after all.

Newquay Certainly does, Mr Redruth.

Polperro (*absently correcting him*) Bodmin.

Bodmin }
Newquay } (*together, triumphantly*) Ha!

Polperro Oh bother!

Dame Come on then, back to *The Grand Pianola*. See if we can't get the old tub off that sandbank.

Smellit Sandbank! What sandbank? What have you done to my ship!

Polperro *My* ship!

Dame Well ... (*She is about to explain, then thinks better of it*) It's a long story. I'll tell you later. Come on, let's go and say hallo to the Navy. And then — England, here we come!

All Hurray!

They troop off

There is a short pause

Cap'n Haddock wanders on, a pick and shovel over one feathered shoulder, the treasure map clutched in his other wingtip

Cap'n Haddock (*scrutinizing the map*) Aaark! Tall tree, Spyglass hill. One hundred paces, Nor', by Nor'-West ... Aaark! Thick as clotted cream! Ha ha ha ha! Pieces of eight! Pieces of eight! Aaark!

He saunters off

CURTAIN

The band strike up a brisk sea march medley. The CURTAIN *rises*

The entire company (except Cap'n Haddock and Slither) are assembled for the grand finalé

Song 13 (Company)

Jim We're bound away for Old England, across the raging foam,

Donna Estella (*to the Dame*) I can't wait to to see your grand hotel, which weel be my new home!

Dame Jim ...

The Dame glares at Jim accusingly. He shrugs, and tries to look innocent

Polperro I'll see you there. After this ruddy trip, I'll have to mortgage the house.

Liversausage Well I'll be glad to get back — for a bottle of sack, and a brace of pot-roast grouse.

Smellit For a brimming jug of black old ale, rare roast beef — and mustard.

Bertha Gunn Fer a teeterin' pile o' cold bread pudden' — and lashin's o' lumpy custard!

Bodmin For peace and quiet, in a sleepy land, where civilized manners are crucial.

Newquay (*reminding Bodmin*) And for a plate of her Fisherman's Pie.

Dame (*nudging Bodmin*) Not to mention a bit of the usual!

Long John Slither enters to join the line-up

Audience participation

Slither I lived my life, a crooked rogue, wi' many a wicked frolic,
     But I never thought that I'd end up, a blessed choc-aholic!

Dame He only got his just desserts — though I must say in concluding,
     I always knew, he'd turn out to be a total chocolate pudding!

Jim We hope you've enjoyed our seafaring tale, and it hasn't been too humdrum,

Dame Now we're bound to the pub for a 'yo ho ho' — and one or two glasses of rum!
     So goodnight, and ——

All   — Merry Christmas! (*or happy new year!*)

Song 14 (Company)

Curtain call

CURTAIN

PRODUCTION NOTES

There is nothing *too* complicated about the staging of this pantomime. As usual, settings can be either as straightforward or as sophisticated as budget and ingenuity permit.

To really maintain the pace of the show however (and specifically to avoid lengthy scene changes), you ideally need two or three different playing areas — probably a raised forestage platform, as well as the stage itself. With this added flexibility, the action may continue in one location, whilst suitably attired stagehands smoothly strike the scenery from the previous scene.

A set of stage blocks or other temporary platform on stage is also useful, providing the bedroom in the inn, the poop deck aboard ship, the raised dais for the stockade, and so on.

There are some further suggestions regarding minor aspects of staging contained within the script itself. Please do not feel obliged to follow the suggested solutions, they are offered as guidance only.

In the original production two temporary 6' x 4' x 4' platforms or "thrusts" were constructed. These were situated on the floor to either side of the stage, projecting towards the audience. The ends of the thrusts facing the audience, together with the void created between them, were faced with a large panel made from hardboard sheets nailed on to a timber frame, which was then lovingly painted as a turbulent seascape. This arrangement created a large "pit" out of view of the audience — but in front of the stage.

This pit was necessary for the plank-walking scene in Act II, Scene 1. The plank (an *extremely* sturdy scaffold board) was pushed out from the stage so that the last two or three feet extended out over the pit. Half a dozen suitably heavy pirates stood foursquare on the "shipboard" end of the plank, to safely counterbalance the victim who edged out over the void — above a comfortable pile of foam rubber crash mats!

A paddling pool was also located in the pit, beside the mats. As each victim jumped off the end of the plank to land in the mats, a crouching member of the stagecrew sent an appropriate splash of water up into the air! (The same trick was used for the cannon ball splash in Act I, Scene 9).

A final word about walking the plank. Please make sure that the actress in the role of Nancy can peep out from underneath her blindfold — otherwise you might lose her overboard sooner than you expect!

The concealed stagehand is also in a position to wield a hardboard cut-out shark's fin on the end of a stick to protrude above the wave caps — greatly exciting younger members of the audience!

The only other moderately challenging aspect is the ship's boat, which we constructed from hardboard planking on a timber frame — although it could quite easily be a two-dimensional cut-out. The boat was located in the pit and placed swiftly on to the thrust, stage left, during a black-out, leaving only the occupants to scramble into position, ready for the lights to come up to the stirring accompaniment of the theme tune to *Hawaii 5-0*, much to the delight of those old enough to remember Jack Lord!

A great deal of fun can be had with this short sequence incidentally, especially with everybody falling about in unison as different occupants of the boat stand up to argue, thereby appearing to rock the boat alarmingly!

The hole in the stage in which the treasure is supposedly buried, and into which Slither ultimately plunges to his doom, is easily accomplished if you are fortunate enough to have a trapdoor in your stage. If not, it should be possible to achieve a similar effect utilizing the pit described above. If all else fails, it's not the end of the world if Slither has to fall back off stage into a pit unseen by the audience.

Last but not least, you need to acquire a seriously large barrel for the apple butt — given that Nancy has to go in head first, but emerge the right way up! If you can't find one large enough, then the fallback is another two-dimensional cut-out!

Wardrobe is generally straightforward, although the pantomime parrot, together with the more opulent costumes for the gentry will probably have to be hired, unless you have a particularly dedicated seamstress amongst your number!

On the plus side, all the pirate costumes are extremely easy to pull together — and the more colourful and outlandish the better!

Lots of nautical and tropical sound effects are required, and these really do help to set the mood for the entire play, so it's important that they are planned and rehearsed properly, not added at the final rehearsal (or first performance) as an afterthought!

Actors portraying the pirate characters are urged to resist the powerful temptation to over-egg the Robert Newton accents, if diction is not to suffer.

One final word of warning, this is a nicely full script. The original production ran out at a whisker over two hours (*not* including the interval). You should aim to keep your performances to this duration.

Most of the lines in the play are one-liners, and should be briskly delivered. This script will work very hard for you if played in the quickfire fashion intended. Guard against over-indulgence. No individual can afford to milk his or her lines, without jeopardizing pace and duration.

FURNITURE AND PROPERTY LIST

ACT I
PROLOGUE

On stage: Upturned barrel. *On it*: lighted candle

SCENE 1

On stage: Inn sign for The Admirable Bimbo Inn
Blackboard

Off stage: Large sea chest (**Billy**)
Tray of steaming fish pies (**Dame**)

Personal: **Jim**: chalk, piece of paper
Billy: cutlass, threepenny bit
Newquay: rolled length of parchment

SCENE 2

On stage: Table. *On it*: tankards
Benches

Personal: **Slither**: cutlass, crutch (used throughout)
Pirates: cutlasses (used throughout)
Blind Puke: white stick (used throughout)

SCENE 3

On stage: Sea chest containing fat purse of coin and map in oilskin packet
Chair
Tankard for **Billy**
Carpet

Off stage: Broom (**Dame**)

Personal: **Billy**: key on string round neck
Pink Dog: cutlass (used throughout)
Blind Puke: two pieces of paper
Pirates: cutlasses

Scene 4

On stage: Table

Scene 5

On stage::   Table
               Benches
               Chair in corner
               Tankards for **Pirates** and **Pink Dog**

Scene 6

On stage: Capstan
               Large barrel

Off stage: Luggage (**Dame**)
               Polperro's trunk (**Bodmin** and **Newquay**)

Personal: **Dame**: jar of pickled eggs

Scene 7

On stage: Capstan
               Large barrel

Off stage: Large crimson feather (**Jim**)
               Apple (**Stage Management**)

Personal: **Slither**: flintlock pistol in belt
               Nancy: clay pipe

Scene 8

On stage: Small table. *On it*: ship's log
               Chairs

Scene 9

On stage: Capstan
               Large barrel
               Skull and crossbones flag
               Muskets and casks of provisions in longboat

Personal: **Dame**: grubby handkerchief

ACT II

SCENE 1

On stage: Capstan
             Large barrel
             Sturdy plank lashed to rail
             Soiled sackcloth
             Muskets and blunderbusses (**Pirates**)

Personal: **Nancy**: blindfolded, hands tied
             Slither: flintlock pistol

SCENE 2

On stage: Palisade with gate. *Behind it*: "coconuts"

Personal: **Polperro**: sword
             Smellit: musket

SCENE 3

On stage: Equatorial foliage

Personal: **Dame**: sweets
             Nancy: sweets
             Bertha Gunn: sweets

SCENE 4

On stage: Bushes

Personal: **Jim**: pistol, knapsack containing sandwiches wrapped in map
             Donna Estella: rope around waist

SCENE 5

On stage: Bushes

Personal: **Polperro**: sword
             Smellit: musket

SCENE 6

On stage: Bushes

Personal: **Donna Estella**: rope
               Jim: rope
               Slither: flintlock pistol
               Smellit: musket

SCENE 7

On stage: Palisade with gate
               Decking section

Off stage: Chocolate covered crutch (**Stage Management**)
               Pick and shovel (**Cap'n Haddock**)

Personal: **Polperro**: sword
               Smellit: musket
               Don Iguana: bandage round head
               Slither: flintlock pistol
               Groundbait: small piece of paper

LIGHTING PLOT

Practical fittings required: candle

Various interior and exterior settings

ACT I, Prologue

To open: Very dim lighting overall, with candle practical and covering spot

Cue 1	Thunder	(Page 1)
	Lightning; snap out candle, fade to black-out	

ACT I, Scene 1

To open: Full general lighting on inn exterior

Cue 2	**Bodmin** stomps off	(Page 7)
	Fade to black-out	

ACT I, Scene 2

To open: Interior lighting

Cue 3	The **Pirates** whoop and leap	(Page 9)
	Fade to black-out	

ACT I, Scene 3

To open: Interior lighting

Cue 4	**Blind Puke** stumbles out	(Page 15)
	Black-out	

ACT I, Scene 4

To open: Interior lighting

Cue 5	**Blind Puke** stumbles out	(Page 16)
	Black-out	

Cue 6   At the end of Song 4   (Page 18)
               Black-out

ACT I, SCENE 5

To open: Interior lighting

Cue 7   The **Pirates** stare at **Nancy** in surprise   (Page 20)
               Black-out

ACT I, SCENE 6

To open: Daylight exterior on deck area

Cue 8   At the end of Song 7   (Page 24)
               Fade to black-out

ACT I, SCENE 7

To open: Daylight exterior on deck area

Cue 9   **Slither** takes bites into the apple   (Page 31)
               Fade to black-out

ACT I, SCENE 8

To open: Interior lighting

Cue 10   **Smellit**: "To the jolly boat!"   (Page 32)
               Fade to black-out

ACT I, SCENE 9

To open: Daylight exterior on deck area

Cue 11   As the skull and crossbones flag is hoisted   (Page 35)
               Cross-fade to longboat area downstage

Cue 12   **Smellit**: "Put up and row!"   (Page 36)
               Cross-fade to deck area

Cue 13   **Slither**: "Ha ha ha!"   (Page 36)
               Cross-fade to longboat area downstage

ACT II, SCENE 1

To open: Daylight exterior on deck area

Cue 14   **Slither** stumps off   (Page 42)
               Fade to black-out

ACT II, SCENE 2

To open: Daylight exterior on stockade

Cue 15   They go off   (Page 45)
               Fade to black-out

ACT II, SCENE 3

To open: Daylight exterior

Cue 16   They exit   (Page 48)
               Fade to black-out

ACT II, SCENE 4

To open: Exterior lighting

Cue 17   They exit   (Page 51)
               Fade to black-out

ACT II, SCENE 5

To open: Daylight exterior

Cue 18   Everyone exits   (Page 53)
               Fade to black-out

ACT II, SCENE 6

To open: Daylight exterior

Cue 19   **Cap'n Haddock** wanders off   (Page 58)
               Fade to black-out

ACT II, SCENE 7

To open: Daylight on stockade area

Cue 20   CURTAIN   (Page 65)
             Cross-fade to full general lighting

EFFECTS PLOT

ACT I

Cue 1   To open   (Page 1)
          Wind howling and rain lashing down; continue throughout
             Prologue

Cue 2   **Slither** laughs   (Page 1)
          Thunder, storm effects

Cue 3   **Nancy**: "The romance ..."   (Page 2)
          Romantic music swells up; cut

Cue 4   **Blind Puke**: "What was that?"   (Page 15)
          Feeble toot on a bugle nearby

Cue 5   **Groundbait** drops his cutlass   (Page 15)
          Horses' hooves fast approaching

Cue 6   **Blind Puke**: "Where are ye, shipmates?"   (Page 15)
          Effect of heavy cavalry regiment at full gallop, increasing in
             volume until end of scene

Cue 7   **Polperro**: " ... only has one leg!"   (Page 17)
          Long, drawn out dramatic chord

Cue 8   **Nancy**: "You can't!"   (Page 18)
          Romantic music swells threateningly

Cue 9   **Polperro** swipes his hand   (Page 18)
          Cut music

Cue 10   Black-out   (Page 20)
          Stirring seafaring music

Cue 11   **Voice**: "Tops'ls away, sir!"   (Page 23)
          Sails flapping and starting to fill with wind

Cue 12   The Lights fade to Black-out   (Page 24)
          Seagulls crying, cordage creaking, timbers groaning,
             waves slooshing, etc.

Cue 13   **Jim**: "Oh Nancy!"   (Page 28)
                Music begins to swell romantically

Cue 14   The **Dame** releases **Nancy**'s legs   (Page 29)
                Cut music

Cue 15   **Smellit**: "To the jolly boat!"   (Page 32)
                Music for scene change

Cue 16   **Groundbait**: "Ay ay, sir!"   (Page 35)
                Dire, portentious music as flag is hoisted

Cue 17   **Polperro**: "Nothing's going to happ——"   (Page 35)
                Ear-splitting bang, followed by deafening scream of flying
                   cannon ball and great splash

Cue 18   **Slither**: "Ha ha ha!"   (Page 36)
                Music; then tropical sound effects as script page 37

ACT II

Cue 19   The **Dame** disappears from view   (Page 40)
                Tremendous splash from below, followed by glugging sound

Cue 20   **Slither**: "What d'ye say, lads?"   (Page 40)
                Loud bleep

Cue 21   **Nancy** jumps   (Page 41)
                Loud splash

Cue 22   The **Pirates** fire   (Page 42)
                Thundering volley of musket shots

Cue 23   The Lights fade to Black-out   (Page 42)
                Music for scene change if requied

Cue 24   **Polperro**: "Up lads and at 'em!"   (Page 44)
                Frantic strumming of Spanish guitars and rattle of castanets

Cue 25   To open SCENE 3   (Page 45)
                Tropical sound effects with waves lapping, etc. as before

Cue 26   **Dame**: "... find Jim and yer pa."   (Page 48)
                Crash of musketry

Cue 27	To open Scene 4	(Page 48)
	Tropical sounds of cicadas, etc.	
Cue 28	**Pink Dog**: "Lay to all hands!"	(Page 54)
	Music	
Cue 29	**Jim**: "What do you mean?"	(Page 62)
	Opening strains of "Rule Britannia"	
Cue 30	**Polperro**: "What's that?"	(Page 62)
	"Rule Britannia" grows louder	
Cue 31	**George Merry**: "Head for the hills!"	(Page 62)
	"Rule Britannia" concludes; "Hearts of Oak" plays	
Cue 32	Curtain; when ready	(Page 65)
	Band plays brisk sea march medley